Happy Father's Day!
Love,
Chris

I hope you have a happy
father's day ☺ love,
Lauren

Natural
Wonders
of
**New
Hampshire**

To a great
daddy,
Your loving
Murp
June 19, 1994

Happy Father's Day!
Love,
Cara

I hope you have a happy
father's day! Love,
Laura.

Natural Wonders

of

New Hampshire

A Guide to Parks, Preserves & Wild Places

Suki Casanave

Illustrated by Lois Stock

Country Roads Press
CASTINE • MAINE

Natural Wonders of New Hampshire
© 1994 by Suki Casanave. All rights reserved.

Published by Country Roads Press
P.O. Box 286, Lower Main Street
Castine, Maine 04421

Text and cover design by Studio 3, Ellsworth, Maine.
Cover photograph courtesy of the New Hampshire Department
   of Resources and Economic Development.
Illustrations by Lois Stock, The Studio, Portland, Maine.
Typesetting by Bill White, Typeworks, Belfast, Maine.

Library of Congress Cataloging-in-Publication Data

Casanave, Suki, 1960–
   Natural wonders of New Hampshire : a guide to parks, preserves,
and open spaces / Suki Casanave ; illustrator, Lois Stock.
      p.   cm.
   Includes bibliographical references and index.
   ISBN 1-56626-043-4 : $9.95
   1. New Hampshire – Guidebooks.   I. Title.
F32.3.C37   1994
   917.4204′43 – dc20   93-37652
                                                                  CIP

Printed in the United States of America.
10 9 8 7 6 5 4 3 2 1

Ye shall go out with joy, and be led forth
with peace: the mountains and the hills shall break
forth before you into singing, and all the trees of
the field shall clap their hands.

— Isaiah 55:12

Contents

Acknowledgments   *xv*
Introduction   *xvii*
To the Reader   *xxi*

1 THE SEACOAST   *1*
Great Bay Estuarine Reserve   2
    Adams Point   2
    Sandy Point   5
Great Bay National Wildlife Refuge   6
Whale-Watching   9
Odiorne Point State Park and Seacoast Science Center   12
Isles of Shoals   15
Fuller Gardens   18
Gardens of the Portsmouth Area   19
    Moffatt-Ladd House   19
    Governor John Langdon House   20
    Rundlet-May House   20
    Wentworth-Coolidge Mansion   20
    Prescott Park   21

Celia Thaxter's Garden 21
Urban Forestry Center 22
East Foss Farm 23
Bellamy River Wildlife Sanctuary 25
Blue Job Mountain 26

2 MONADNOCK REGION **27**
Meetinghouse Pond 28
Mount Monadnock 29
A Trio of Little Mountains 31
    Pitcher Mountain 31
    Bald Mountain 31
    Gap Mountain 33
Pisgah State Park 33
Rhododendron State Park 34
Miller State Park 35
Wapack National Wildlife Refuge 36
Sheiling State Forest 39
Heald Tract 40
McCabe Forest 41
Harris Center for Conservation Education 42
Peirce Wildlife and Forest Reservation 45
Madame Sherri Forest 47

3 MERRIMACK VALLEY **49**
Ponemah Bog 50
Deering Wildlife Sanctuary 51
Fox State Forest 53
Robert Frost Farm 54
Amoskeag Fishway 55
Silk Farm Wildlife Sanctuary and Audubon Center 56
Merrimack River Outdoor Education Area and
    Conservation Center 59
Christa McAuliffe Planetarium 61

Bear Brook State Park 62
Pawtuckaway State Park 63
Northwood Meadows Pioneer Park 64

4 LAKES REGION 67

Squam Lakes Area 68
Unsworth Preserve 68
Chamberlain-Reynolds Forest 69
Moon and Bowman Islands 70
West and East Rattlesnake 71
Five-Finger Point 72
Eagle Cliff and Red Hill 72
Science Center of New Hampshire 73

Winnipesaukee Area 74
Stonedam Island Natural Area 74
Frederick and Paula Anna Markus Sanctuary 76
Kimball Wildlife Forest 77
Belknap Mountain 78
Knight's Pond 79

Lakes Region East 81
Hoyt Wildlife Sanctuary 81
Thompson Bird Sanctuary and Wildlife Refuge 83
Frank Bolles Nature Reserve 84
White Lake State Park 86
West Branch Pine Barrens 88

5 DARTMOUTH–
LAKE SUNAPEE REGION 90
John Hay National Wildlife Refuge 91
Stoney Brook Wildlife Sanctuary 95
Pillsbury State Park 95

Mount Sunapee State Park   96
Mount Kearsarge   99
Philbrick-Cricenti Bog   100
Saint-Gaudens National Historic Site   101
Helen Woodruff Smith Sanctuary   105
Mount Cardigan   106
Paradise Point Nature Center   107

6 WHITE MOUNTAINS   *110*

White Mountains South   *111*
Sandwich Range Wilderness Area   111
    Mount Chocorua   113
    Big Rock Cave   114
    Mount Israel   114
    Sandwich Notch Road   115
Waterville Valley Area   117
    Welch and Dickey Mountains 117
    East Pond   118
    The Scaur   119
    Jennings Peak   119

White Mountains Central   *120*
Kancamagus Highway Area   120
    Bear Notch Road   120
    Table Mountain   121
    Hedgehog Mountain and Mount Potash 121
    East Branch Truck Road   122
    Boulder Loop Interpretive Trail 123
    Greeley Ponds Scenic Area 123
Crawford Notch Area   125
    Elephant Head   126
    Ammonoosuc Lake   126
    Lower Ammonoosuc Falls   127

Mount Avalon   127
Caps Ridge Trail   128
Zealand Notch   128
Mount Jackson   130
Mount Crawford   131
Mount Carrigain   132

White Mountains West   *134*
Franconia Notch Area   134
    Mount Pemigewasset   135
    Georgiana Falls   135
    Basin-Cascade Trail and Lonesome Lake   136
    The Franconia Bike Path and the Rim Trail 137
Moosilauke and Kinsman Notch Area   137
    Mount Moosilauke   138
    Black Mountain   139
    Tunnel Brook   139
    Wachipauka Pond   140
    Beaver Brook Cascades   141
    Road through Kinsman Notch   141
    Lost River Reservation   142

White Mountains East   *144*
Pinkham Notch Area   144
    Square Ledge   146
    Glen Boulder   147
    Imp Profile   147
    Carter Notch   149
North Conway Area   149
    Mount Kearsarge North   150
    Mountain Pond   151
    Black Cap   151
    Peaked Mountain (Green Hills Preserve) 152
Evans Notch Area   154

Deer Hill Bog Wildlife Viewing Blind 155
Little Deer Hill and Big Deer Hill 155
The Basin 156
South Baldface and Eastman Mountains 156

White Mountains North 157
Randolph Area 157
    Pine Mountain 158
    Dome Rock 162
    Lookout Ledge 162
    King Ravine 163

7 THE NORTH COUNTRY 166
Southwest Corner 167
    Weeks State Park 167
    The Rocks 168
    Bretzfelder Memorial Park 170
    Pondicherry 171
Mahoosuc Range 172
    Mascot Pond 173
    Mount Hayes 175
    Mount Success 176
    Thirteen-Mile Woods 176
Kilkenny Region 177
    Devil's Hopyard 177
    South Pond 178
    Rogers Ledge 179
    Unknown Pond and the Horn 179
    Kilkenny Ridge 180
Nash Stream State Forest 181
    Percy Peaks 181
    Sugarloaf Mountain 182
Lake Umbagog National Wildlife Refuge 182
    Diamond Peaks 184

Dixville Notch   185
    Table Rock   186
    Sanguinary Ridge   186
Connecticut Lakes Region   188
    Scott Bog and East Inlet   189
    Magalloway Mountain   192
    Garfield Falls   193
    Fourth Connecticut Lake   194

Appendix: For More Information   *195*
          Maps, Guides, and Books   *198*
Index   *203*

Acknowledgments

First, thanks should go to all the individuals and "green organizations" working to protect New Hampshire's land. Without them, this book could not have been written.

Thanks especially to David Anderson and Geoff Jones at the Society for the Protection of New Hampshire Forests; Stephen Walker at the Audubon Society of New Hampshire; Patrick McCarthy and Krista Helmboldt at The Nature Conservancy; Buzz Durham and Dave Govatski of the White Mountain National Forest; Brian Fowler at the Mount Washington Observatory; Tom Howe of the Lakes Region Conservation Trust; and Sarah Thorne, former land negotiator for the Land Conservation Investment Program.

Peter Benson, Gene Daniell, Mike Dickerman, Joe Gill, Doug Mayer, Libby Morse, Vinny Spiotti, and Dana Steele generously contributed their knowledge of the mountains. So did countless other hikers I met along the trails who added their suggestions and favorite places. Special thanks to Steven Smith, who knows New Hampshire's peaks in every season and willingly shared his expertise and editorial advice. Thanks to Dawn Cadey and Kathleen Brandes for their editing.

And finally, thanks to my family, who watched this project take shape and cheered its completion. This book is dedicated to you — and to everyone who loves the green spaces of New Hampshire.

Introduction

Conservation is a state of harmony
between men and the land.

— Aldo Leopold, *A Sand County Almanac*

Certain things you never forget: watching the mist shift and settle across a northern bog ringed with fir trees; an expanse of salt marsh gone purple with autumn; a dark flock of Canada geese rising in raucous unison against a slate sky. Small things, too, stay with you: wild columbine at a bend in the trail; the sound of frogs flopping into a still pond; the endless song of a winter wren in a midsummer forest; standing face-to-face with a moose.

This book is about moments like these — moments seen and heard along New Hampshire's mountain ledges and watery shores, in open fields and deep boreal forests. It's a book that could be written because countless people and "green organizations," large and small, have worked and bargained and negotiated and fought — for the land. Without their efforts, which have spanned more than a century, New Hampshire today would look very different.

As of September 1993, just under 20 percent of the state's nearly six million acres had been saved from development. The White Mountain National Forest's 770,000 acres constitute about two thirds of this protected land (about 13 percent of the total state land). The remaining one third of the saved land (about 7 percent of the total state land) is scattered in parcels large and small around the state. Some of these acres were saved, in the eleventh hour, from certain development. Many were given outright to conservation organizations. Others are privately owned, permanently protected by conservation easements.

This book is an invitation to visit some of these places – to walk the trails, paddle the waters, appreciate the views, learn about the habitats. It is, essentially, a book about the protected one-fifth of the state. And so, it raises a question: What about the rest of New Hampshire's land?

According to the New Hampshire Office of State Planning, somewhere between 3.5 and 6 percent of the state is considered developed, depending on how you define *developed*. That leaves roughly 75 percent of the state that is both undeveloped and unprotected. That's an awful lot of distance between sanctuary signs – imagine what the state would look like if all that unprotected land were developed.

The vision of a state overrun by development was precisely what fueled the Land Conservation Investment Program (LCIP), which began in 1987. By the time it finished in the spring of 1993, the amount of protected state land had nearly doubled – from about 120,000 acres to about 200,000. "We had applications on well over three times the amount of land we could serve," says LCIP land negotiator Sarah Thorne. "There's lots more out there that deserves protection and that people are willing to protect. The question now is, 'How do we save more land?' "

The issues are complex, the questions difficult. How do we balance the demands of growth and the need for land protection? What level of protection is appropriate? Can we sustain a traditional "working landscape" that includes farming and logging – and still meet the growing demand for public access to the land? We must consider all these things. But before we can achieve the harmony between man and the land that legendary naturalist Aldo Leopold suggests is possible, we must, above all, feel an affinity for the earth. If we don't love it, we won't protect it. This book will not answer the hard questions. It will, I hope, help you learn more about the land. Most of all, I hope you will find in these pages places that you love.

To the Reader

Some of the most beautiful places in New Hampshire are ones you have never heard of – places set aside, often with tremendous effort on the part of many individuals, in order to protect the land. The purpose of this book is to take you to some of these places, as well as to revisit some better-known spots. The organizations and individuals who own and manage these protected acres – large and small, well-known and obscure – agreed to be included here. (A list of New Hampshire's "green organizations" appears on page 195.)

Their desire is not to have their property overrun by visitors, but they do want the land to be appreciated – to be open to thoughtful, respectful users. They know that the best way to save more land is to provide others with the opportunity to see its beauty up close. Whether you're hiking a 4,000-footer or strolling through a patch of lady's slippers, please keep in mind the effort that goes into land protection. Be a careful, quiet, "low-impact" user and leave no mark of your presence.

The emphasis in this book is on walking and hiking, although you'll also find ponds and lakes to canoe, bike trails to ride, and good spots to camp. But the real focus is on the places themselves — their beauty, as well as their natural history, wildlife, and geology. These "eco-details" throughout the book fill you in on, among other things, bats and bogs, eagles and cirques — and even felsenmeer creeps.

The text, organized by regions, takes you, roughly, south to north through New Hampshire. Below is some useful information to consider before you go. I wish you many happy "green" adventures.

Sanctuaries and Preserves. Generally, trails on these lands tend to be flat walking trails, one to three miles long, that make ideal half-day excursions. Many of these refuges have maps and/or nature trail guides available, either at the trailheads or from the organization that owns and manages the property.

The best available overview of lands protected by the Forest Society — officially the Society for the Preservation of New Hampshire Forests (SPNHF) — is its lands map, which includes brief descriptions of many of the Forest Society properties ($4.95, plus $1.50 for shipping and handling).

The Audubon Society of New Hampshire (ASNH) prints educational trail guides that are found in mailboxes at the start of most of their trails. You can also write their Silk Farm headquarters in Concord for information (guides cost fifty cents).

All the sanctuaries and preserves in this book, regardless of ownership, are fragile places. They are designed only for travel on foot (and, in some cases, by canoe). No motor vehicles, campfires, hunting, trapping, or fishing is allowed, unless otherwise specified. Please do not remove or destroy plants or wildlife. Dogs may visit SPNHF and ASNH lands, but please keep them on a leash and pick up after them. Dogs are discouraged on lands belonging to The Nature Conservancy (TNC). Keep in mind that most SPNHF land includes working forest. Do not block access roads.

State Parks. Trail maps to state parks are available at each park. Most parks charge a small admission fee in-season. Please practice a carry-in, carry-out policy. Dogs are allowed in many of the parks and most campgrounds, but never on state beaches or in the water.

Watching Wildlife. "Most people just want to get close enough to see," says Steve Breeser, manager of the Lake Umbagog National Wildlife Refuge, one of the richest areas for wildlife in the state. "Take loons, for instance – people will pull up as close as they can in a boat and think all they're doing is looking. But they'll chase away the adults and leave the babies exposed, which is the worst possible thing you could do." The best thing you could do is to use binoculars. And keep a respectful distance. Be still and wait.

A Word about the White Mountains and the North Country

Remember that courage and strength are naught without prudence.
Do nothing in haste, look well to each step and from the beginning think what may be the end.

> – Edward Whymper, nineteenth-century mountaineer

New Hampshire's northern regions are famous for their drama and beauty. They are also famous for their harsh weather and treacherous terrain. As you head out to explore this area, give careful consideration to your preparation.

Before You Go. Assemble all of the equipment and information you will need. Call the district ranger station. Ask about trail conditions. Ask for maps. Listen to a weather report, and let a friend know where you are going. Then make sure you have the basic supplies listed below. (If you are planning an overnight, you'll need more.)

- Sturdy hiking boots
- Trail map
- Extra food and water
- Extra clothing
- Flashlight

- First-aid kit
- Matches
- Pocketknife
- Whistle
- Compass

Respecting the mountains, learning about their harsh conditions, and preparing for them will help you enjoy your hikes. Ultimately, you are responsible for your own safety. And wisdom is your best guide.

Minimizing Your Impact. Even the most careful, well-intentioned hiker has some impact on the environment. You can help to minimize the effects of your presence by following these guidelines and using thoughtful common sense as you go. (If you are planning on camping, get the *Backcountry Camping* guide from a ranger station.)

- Hike in small groups.
- Stay on the trail.
- Camp at least 200 feet from any trail or water source.
- Use stoves instead of fires.
- Adopt a "no-trace" ethic, naturalizing campsites before leaving.
- Carry out your trash; pick up trash left by others.
- Bury human waste in a "cat hole."

Distances, Times, and Maps. The trail descriptions in the White Mountains and North Country chapters include a one-way distance (to the summit) and an approximate time based on a standard calculation: a half hour for each mile and for each 1,000 feet climbed. (Thus, a one-mile trip up a 1,000-foot mountain would take an hour.)

These calculations are intended only as guidelines – and as a reminder to those new to the mountains that climbing a mile is not the same as walking a mile. But everyone's pace is different, and you'll need to work out your own estimates. No matter where you are going, be sure to go with map in hand (see list of maps, guides, and books on page 198). Call the district ranger station for up-to-date information on conditions before you go.

Accessibility. The White Mountain National Forest publishes information about the accessibility of many day-use and overnight recreation facilities, as well as trails, in the forest. The list includes descriptions of grades, rest-room facilities, and other potential obstacles for about fifty campgrounds and trails. *Contact WMNF, P.O. Box 638, 719 Main Street, Laconia, NH 03246; 603-528-8721; TTY 603-528-8722.*

Paper-Company Land. Most of New Hampshire's northernmost land is privately owned. In the Connecticut Lakes region, about 75 percent of the acreage belongs to Champion International; other big landowners include Boise-Cascade, New England Power Company, and Perry Stream Land and Timber. Under the current open-land policy, these forests are open for public day use at no charge, but their primary purpose is to grow and harvest timber.

On the narrow gravel roads that run through this commercial woodland, logging trucks have the right-of-way. As you drive, be alert for oncoming vehicles and proceed with extreme caution. There are no road signs or stop signs, no curve signs or speed limits. Roads are generally not maintained in winter, and some are closed during the spring mud season. No camping, fires, or ATVs are permitted on this land.

1

The Seacoast

*In the recurrent rhythms of tides and surf
and in the varied life of the tide lines, there is the
obvious attraction of movement and change
and beauty. There is also, I am convinced, a deeper
fascination born of inner meaning and significance.*
— Rachel Carson, *The Edge of the Sea*

Ever since the spring of 1990, members of the Great Bay Watch have been keeping an eye on New Hampshire's estuary waters. Twice a month, from March through November, dozens of volunteers head for riverbanks and beaches, slippery docks and salt marshes. Carrying collecting buckets, pH meters, hydrometers, and thermometers, they take samples and test for, among other things, salinity, turbidity, and temperature. They conduct dissolved-oxygen tests in the backs of their cars. Their findings support the work of scientists who are studying Great Bay, examining the water, the mud, and the microscopic particles that make up this estuarine ecosystem.

The Great Bay Watch volunteers are learning about the

ecological complexities in these seacoast waters. They are looking at things the rest of us observe only indirectly: a heron pulls
an eel from the mud; an eagle dives for a fish; a whale swims
after copepods. These animals, and countless others, depend
directly on what happens in the mudflats and around the edges of
the salt marshes. In New Hampshire's crowded seacoast region,
where development continues to bear down on every fragile
edge, the "recurrent rhythms of tides and surf" have something to
teach us. The sea draws us to its beauty. We walk its shores,
watch its shifting light, turn our faces toward its salty breeze.
Gradually, we must learn from it.

GREAT BAY ESTUARINE RESERVE

This inland bay includes 4,471 acres of tidal waters and mudflats
and forty-eight miles of shoreline, as well as 800 protected acres
of salt marshes, tidal creeks, woodlands, and open fields. The
public can visit Great Bay at Adams Point and Sandy Point (both
part of the reserve) and at the Great Bay National Wildlife
Refuge (see page 6).

Adams Point

Adams Point, the site of the Jackson Estuarine Research Laboratory, offers bird-watching and quiet strolling by the bay.

Directions: From State 108 S in Durham, turn left onto Durham
Point Road. Follow it for three miles and turn left through the
gate onto the point. Drive to the end of the road and park.

On a breezy summer morning, Adams Point is noisy with
bird calls. A flicker sweeps from a nearby bush, his flight path
quick and undulating. Blossoms loosen and drift on the breeze.
Fields of grass bend and straighten, shifting under the wind like
the sea itself.

Wade first through this green sea, down and then up along a tiny path, grass brushing at your waist. Push on, a little farther across wide-open meadow, and then, there it is — Great Bay, a brilliant expanse shimmering under the summer sun.

This bit of sea is actually an estuary, where freshwater rivers and ocean tides come together, supplying nutrients and shelter for some twenty-three species of threatened or endangered animals and plants — including, in winter, the bald eagle (see box). As many as twenty of these great birds have been sighted in a single season, drawn by the waters in the channel of the bay, kept open by shifting tides. In summer, glossy ibis and

---

BALD EAGLES IN NEW HAMPSHIRE

"Most people don't realize that the best time to see eagles in New Hampshire is in the winter," says Diane DeLuca, senior biologist for the Audubon Society of New Hampshire (ASNH), who estimates that seventy to seventy-five of these federally listed endangered birds overwinter in the state. The eagles come south, mostly from Canada, in search of two things: food and roosting sites. They find both along the Merrimack River and on the seacoast's Great Bay. "Great Bay is an especially good place for them," says DeLuca, "because there are so many overwintering waterfowl, an important food source."

The best spot to watch for eagles is on Adams Point, about a half hour after sunrise. From here you can see across the water to the dead tree on Woodman Point at the Great Bay National Wildlife Refuge. Eagles spend much of the day in this "perch tree," surveying the water. When they fly, they lift themselves from the tree with wings that spread six to eight feet across. In the late afternoon, the birds return to roosting sites just south of Adams Point. Deep in the bushy branches of these white pines, the birds are safe from harsh winter weather.

You can help with the Bald Eagle Project by reporting any eagle sightings to the ASNH or to the New Hampshire Fish and Game Department.

---

snowy egrets wade at the water's edge, and the belted king-fisher dives for food. In autumn, the Canada geese return. Huge flocks of up to 1,000 rise from the bay all at once, as if to some

Bald eagles winter on New Hampshire's coast

soundless command. The fury of their flapping and honking as they lift into the air lingers long after they have disappeared over the horizon.

Adams Point is an eighty-acre, rock-lined peninsula that divides Great Bay to the south from Little Bay to the north. Once the site of the Adams family farm, the property has also supported a hotel, a brickyard, and a shipyard at different times in its history. Today, Jackson Lab, a nationally known estuarine research laboratory, sits on the site of the old Adams House. Here research scientists from the University of New Hampshire keep watch over the bay, studying its ecology and productivity, investigating pollution sources and water quality. The handicapped-accessible observation platform is an ideal site for birdwatching all year and for eagle-watching in winter (when not covered by heavy snow).

To do: *walking, bird-watching. Contact the New Hampshire Fish and Game Department, 225 Main Street, Durham, NH 03824; 603-868-1095.*

Sandy Point
A 1,600-foot boardwalk and an indoor interpretive center introduce visitors to the salt-marsh habitat of Great Bay. (The graded gravel path and boardwalk are accessible to those with limited mobility.)

Directions: From State 101 in Stratham, take the second left after the Squamscott Road light onto Depot Road. Follow it to the end and turn left. Cross the tracks to the parking area.

Discover an autumn-blooming plant with a funny name and a species of grass that can secrete salt through its roots. Watch for redwing blackbirds in the cattails, or, at low tide, gaze out across 2,000 feet of mudflats. Unlike the rocky coast of Adams Point, Sandy Point is Great Bay's prime salt-marsh area. It is here among the grasses that the most fertile ecosystem in the world has its roots. As these plants die and decompose, they release nutrients that are washed out to sea.

The marsh also acts as a valuable sponge, protecting surrounding land from flooding. As you walk the boardwalk, a trail guide tells you more about what makes the bay so "great." Be on the lookout for northern harriers, osprey, and great blue herons. At the indoor interpretive center, kids can pick up horseshoe crabs and other salt-marsh life from the touch tank. A model of Great Bay explains the estuary's history.

To do: marshwalk, bird-watching; educational programs. Contact the New Hampshire Fish and Game Department, 225 Main Street, Durham, NH 03824; 603-868-1095.

GREAT BAY NATIONAL WILDLIFE REFUGE

This 1,054-acre refuge, once part of Pease Air Force Base, borders 6.5 miles of shoreline on Great Bay.

Directions: From the Spaulding Turnpike, drive three miles west of Portsmouth to the Pease International Tradeport exit in Newington. Follow Merrimack Road to the McIntyre Road overpass at the entrance to the refuge. The refuge road continues to the old Margeson estate, where trails begin. (Opening scheduled for 1994.)

The most famous tree in the Great Bay National Wildlife Refuge is a dead one. The seventy-foot white pine stands alone, stark and white against the sky, a favorite winter roosting spot for bald eagles. Woodman Point Trail, which leads to the tree, is closed in winter (to protect the eagles from disturbance), but you can watch for the federally listed endangered birds from the Turner Loop Trail, which also winds through this corner of the refuge. In warmer weather, the half-mile walk to the "eagle tree" is worth a trip in itself—the waters of Great Bay lap against the shore only feet from the trail. In all, five miles of trails are planned at the refuge, much of them along the water's edge.

These protected waters also attract common loon, osprey, common terns, and harriers (marsh hawks), as well as the endangered peregrine falcon. Bird-watchers might spot smaller birds during summer — warblers, scarlet tanagers, indigo buntings — neotropical migrants that summer in North America and winter in South America (see box, page 64). Raptors settle here during breeding season: kestrels and red-tailed hawks, as well as screech and great horned owls. And then there's the wild turkey, whose ungainly profile is one of the most common sights in the refuge.

The list of wildlife goes on: coyote, red and gray fox, white-tailed deer; more birds, fish, mammals. And that's the whole point of this place — to provide a refuge for wildlife. But it wasn't always quite this way. Until 1989, the area was better known as Pease Air Force Base, and even though the refuge has always been a conservation area, reminders of man's presence are never far away: Before reaching the trails, visitors must drive past a fenced-in weapons-storage area. The squat cement buildings, along with fifteen underground bunkers, are empty now, but planes still roar overhead, as Pease begins its new life as a commercial airport.

Thankfully, the land to the west of the landing strip — 1,054 acres — has been preserved for wildlife. And for limited use by the public. Eventually, even the ugly storage area will be put to good use: One of the bunkers will be used as a bat cave; a low depression in the middle, once a pond, will be reflooded to attract birds; the chain-link fence will protect nesting birds from skunks and raccoons; even the many floodlight posts, linked by a maze of electrical wires, may someday serve as perching and nesting spots for osprey and other raptors.

To do: hiking, wildlife observation, cross-country skiing. Contact the U.S. Fish and Wildlife Service, 601 Spaulding Turnpike, Suite 17, Portsmouth, NH 03801; 603-431-7511.

WHAT IS AN ESTUARY? THE STORY OF GREAT BAY

Great Bay is a place where the rivers really do "run down to the sea" — eventually. The Winnicut, Lamprey, and Squamscott rivers all flow directly into the bay. But Great Bay does not open, like most bays, directly into the ocean. "What really makes Great Bay unique," says reserve manager Peter Wellenberger, "is that you have to travel from the ocean more than ten miles, up the Piscataqua River and through Little Bay, before you even get to it. It's the largest inland bay on the East Coast — so far inland, many people think it's fresh water." In fact, the salt level in the bay shifts dramatically, depending on the time of year; spring runoff can be so great that the bay fills almost entirely with fresh water.

The history of the bay began a million years ago, when a glacier compressed the land to a level about forty feet lower than it is today. As the tremendous weight receded, the land began to rebound. But Great Bay and adjacent Little Bay bounced back more slowly, leaving a sag in the surface. "It was just the right set of circumstances that allowed the river to flood it and connect it to the sea," says Wellenberger. As this depression was filled by mud and water transported by the rising sea level, it created the unusual "drowned river valley"-type estuary called "Great Bay." Except for Furber Strait, which is about fifty-eight feet deep where it runs past Adams Point, most of the bay is only eight to ten feet deep.

Today, the sea flows in and out of Great Bay twice a day, coming and going through Little Bay and the Piscataqua River. The other three rivers bring nutrients into the bay; each six-to-eight-foot tide redistributes them to coastal waters in an ongoing cycle that is the foundation of a complex ecosystem. "Estuaries are called 'nurseries of the sea,'" explains Wellenberger. "Their productivity per square foot is just immense. Two-thirds of all the commercially caught fish in the world have some connection to an estuary — they were born there or eat something from there." The great whales themselves could not survive without the microscopic nutrients flushed from the salt marshes (see entry on page 9).

Great Bay itself provides a banquet for countless birds and wildlife. Striped bass spend the summer feeding on minnows, silversides, and smelt that live in the estuary, migrating back to Chesapeake Bay for the winter. Herons prey on fish and eels. Sandpipers and plovers search the mud for shrimp, small crabs, and amphipods that live in the sediment. Local fishermen pull flounder, striped bass, bluefish, and lobsters from these waters.

"This estuary is especially rich in oysters," says Rich Langan, a zoologist at Jackson Lab, "and shellfishing depends on clean water." Because oysters are filter feeders, they, like other shellfish, are especially susceptible to pollution, and most of Great Bay's shellfish beds are currently closed due to pollution. In recent years, surrounding cities have been upgrading their sewage-treatment plants, but that accounts for only part of the problem, according to Langan. "If you have inadequate septic systems, it doesn't take very many homes and people to degrade the water quality to the point where you can't take shellfish." As the cleanup continues, someday shellfishing may return throughout the waters of Great Bay.

WHALE-WATCHING
Whale-watching vessels go out to sea in search of giant mammals and lessons about marine life.

Directions: Cruises leave from Rye and downtown Portsmouth. Call for directions (see page 12).

The whales that swim along New Hampshire's coast rise and fall through the dark sea, water spilling from their magnificent backs. Sometimes they are accompanied by pods of dolphins, twenty or forty leaping and diving escorts who catch a free ride on the bow waves that roll off the great creatures. Occasionally a humpback whale rises with a great sweep of energy, breaking through the water with a primitive grace. "They may 'breach' to remove barnacles," says one naturalist, "which can accumulate on their chins in masses of up to a ton, but nobody's sure exactly why they do it."

The forty-five-foot humpbacks are popular, but the giant finbacks are favorites of New Hampshire Seacoast Cruises' Captain Leo Axton: "If you can swing in alongside a finback — that's a massive experience," he says. At about a ton per foot, finbacks weigh seventy tons, roughly equivalent to thirty-five full-size automobiles. Each lung itself is about the size of a compact car — large enough to seat four. Considered the only consistently asymmetrically marked mammal in the world, finbacks have a jaw that is white on the right side. Although they don't breach, these massive creatures occasionally perform chin slams, lunging out of the water and slapping back down with a shuddering thwack.

Whales swim these waters in search of food, which they often find along the ledges — submerged mountain ranges, really — where tremendous upwellings create prime feeding

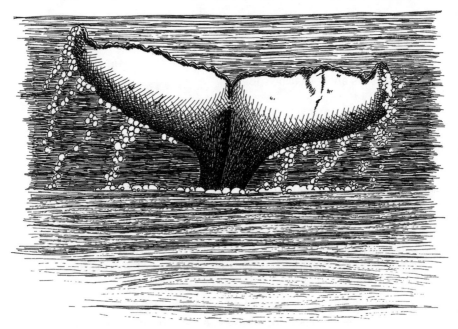

A humpback whale dives

SUMMER BIRDING TIP: HEAD OUT TO SEA

One of the best ways to watch birds on the seacoast in summer is to take a whale-watching cruise — and keep your eyes on the sky as well as on the water. The open sea provides the best chance of spotting the pelagic birds you'd never be able to see from shore. Described by the Greek *pelagos,* meaning "sea," these birds spend their entire lives over the ocean. Watch for the greater shearwater, the sooty shearwater, and the little Wilson's storm petrel, which looks something like a swallow. This tiny bird nests near Antarctica, laying its single egg in a burrow in the ground, then returning at night to feed its young. It spends its summers in the Northern Hemisphere, usually in huge flocks of up to several thousand.

Like St. Peter, whose name it shares, the petrel walks on water — or seems to. When feeding, it patters across the surface of the water, wings outstretched, searching for planktonic copepods. Petrels, like shearwaters, are specially adapted to be able to drink salt water, secreting excess salt through their salt glands. Look for flocks of petrels directly behind a swimming whale. The tiny birds "walk" along in the wake, feeding on organisms brought to the surface by the giant tail as it rises and falls, propelling the whale through the water.

---

grounds. When deep currents hit the bottoms of these ledges, there's nowhere to go but up. As the water rises, it carries nutrients that the tides washed to the ocean floor from the salt marshes. Swept to the surface, where photosynthesis takes place, plankton develops. The small crustaceans called copepods, which feed on the plankton, are a favorite food of some whales.

When they come up from feeding to breathe, every three to eight minutes, the massive mammals send up a spout of water. Humpbacks spew in wide, bushy bursts; finbacks shoot long, narrow columns up to thirty feet. On a whale watch, all eyes are on the water, searching for telltale spouts, though sightings are never guaranteed.

The best time for a whale-watching cruise is mid-July to mid-September. For cruise times and prices, contact N.H. Sea-coast Cruises, Route 1A (P.O. Box 232), Rye, NH 03870; 800-734-6488; or Isles of Shoals Steamship Co. (ISSCO), Barker Wharf, 315 Market Street, Portsmouth, NH 03801; 800-894-5509 (in NH); 800-441-4620.

ODIORNE POINT STATE PARK
and SEACOAST SCIENCE CENTER

This indoor-outdoor glimpse of the sea includes seven different habitats on more than 300 acres, several miles of trails, abundant bird life, and plenty of history and nature lessons.

Directions: Take the main entrance to Odiorne Point State Park, just off State 1A in Rye.

History looms at the entrance to Odiorne Point State Park, a hulking mound of earth at the edge of the parking lot. During World War II, this summer resort community became Fort Dearborn. Homes were torn down and giant concrete casements were built and camouflaged beneath hillocks of earth and trees. Today the Seacoast Science Center stands just beyond one of these casements on the site of Odiorne's last summer residence.

In the exhibit area, you can plunge your hands into the chilly water of the touch tank and withdraw palm-size sea stars or tiny leg-waving crabs. At the "Indoor Walk" exhibit, you can pick up bits and pieces of treasures collected along Odiorne Point's wrack line (high-tide line): giant chunks of lobster shell, horseshoe crab shells, even a dolphin skull. Everything is smooth and hard, polished by the sea.

At the Gulf of Maine tank, you can try to spot a winter flounder, whose unremarkable name is as deceptive as its looks. This creature is a Picasso painting come to life. By some odd miracle of nature, its left eye migrates to the other side of its body; it can also change color along its right side. Flattening itself, left side down, into the sand, it becomes invisible. Keep watching, and you'll soon notice fish-shaped chunks of shifting "sand" — the only clues are the two bulbous eyes crowded close together.

Outside, along New Hampshire's last stretch of undeveloped rocky coastline, you can go tidepooling with one of the center's naturalists. Or walk to the salt marsh at the northern end of the park and watch for herons and egrets, lean and gaunt among the tall grasses. Shorebirds, too, flock to this feeding ground at low tide — sandpipers, plover, terns, plus greater and lesser yellowlegs, stabbing their sharp bills into the salty muck.

The diversity of habitats within the park makes it an ideal spot for botanists as well as birders: More than 400 flowering plants have been identified here. Trails meander through the woods, past overgrown stone walls and, in one spot, the remains of a formal garden — ghostly reminders of the grand homes that once stood along the point. In the perennial gardens near the Science Center blooms the apothecary rose, thought to be the oldest rose in this part of the country.

Close to the water, the trail winds beneath twisted stands of staghorn sumac, named for the velvety touch of its stems, similar to the horns of a deer. Its woody branches emerge from the earth like giant clusters of horns. The paved bike path provides wheelchair access past the pond to the salt marsh. And in winter, if snow falls, the trails are open to cross-country skiers, who can glide along by the sea.

To do: walking, biking, bird-watching, tidepooling, picnicking, cross-country skiing; nature store; educational programs throughout the year for families, children, and adults. The Seacoast Science Center at Odiorne Point State Park is managed by the Audubon Society of New Hampshire under contract with the state, in affiliation with the Friends of Odiorne Point and the

WINTER BIRDING TIP: WALK THE BEACH

In winter, the beaches along New Hampshire's seventeen miles of coastline lie gray and deserted. But this windswept terrain, empty of tourists, is filled with birds. Steve Mirick, president of the Seacoast chapter of the Audubon Society of New Hampshire and birder extraordinaire, offers these tips on what to see and where to see it, heading south to north along US 1 and State 1A.

At *Hampton Beach,* look for snowy owls sitting on the bathhouses. They summer in the arctic tundra and spend the winter here, feeding in open, grassy areas. You'll also find horned larks and snow buntings around the parking area. Snow buntings, whose winter plumage is not as vibrant as their stark black-and-white summer dress, are the whitest of all songbirds. Their flashing white wing patches identify them in flight.

Because it juts out into the ocean, *Rye Harbor State Park* is a good spot to watch for black-legged kittiwakes, gannets, and other pelagics — those birds that spend their lives above the ocean and are rarely glimpsed from land. Kittiwakes and gannets nest farther north on rocky offshore cliffs and spend the winter here. You'll also find two ducks: barrow's and common goldeneye, their purple-and-green heads glinting in the winter sun.

Odiorne Point is the place for winter ducks, which fly south in search of open water: the common eider, the white-winged scooter, horned and red-necked grebes, common and red-throated loons, the red-breasted merganser. If you're lucky, you may see a flock of oldsquaw — and hear them, a floating mass of black and white, sending up their laughing cry across the water.

Portsmouth Harbor is home to several varieties of gulls: glaucous, Iceland, sometimes even the rare black-headed or ivory gull. The black-headed gull, which loses its chocolate-brown hood in winter, is formerly from Europe and only started occurring off our coast in the last couple of decades. "The ivory gull is so rare around here, it's only been spotted twice in the last decade," says Mirick. This small, white bird with a yellow-tipped black bill spends most of its life around pack ice, feeding on polar bear kills and seal dung. "If an ivory were spotted," says Mirick, "you'd see bird-watchers from all over the East coming to see it."

Herring gull chick just out of its shell

University of New Hampshire Cooperative Extension/Sea Grant Program. Small fee charged for the park in-season; Science Center is free (donations appreciated). Contact SSC, P.O. Box 674, Rye, NH 03870; 603-436-8043.

ISLES OF SHOALS
Nine rocky islands off the coast of New Hampshire have weathered the sea for centuries.

Directions: Isles of Shoals (ISSCO) cruises leave from Barker

Wharf — as well as from two other locations (see page 17). From I-95, take Exit 7 toward downtown Portsmouth.

The M/V *Thomas Laighton* pulls out of Portsmouth Harbor at 11 A.M. every day, all summer long — beneath the drawbridge, past the hulking metal skyline of the Portsmouth Naval Shipyard, past Portsmouth Harbor Light, toward the open sea. When the Isles of Shoals first appear on the horizon, ten miles from the harbor, they look, in the words of author Celia Thaxter, "barren, bleak and bare . . . mere heaps of granite in the wide and lonely sea." But Thaxter, who spent most of her nineteenth-century life here on these islands, saw in the "wildness and desolation . . . a strange beauty."

Today the island cluster looks much as it always has, dotted here and there with buildings, stripped of all but necessity. On little White Island, where Celia Thaxter grew up, there is only the lighthouse where her father, Thomas Laighton, once served as keeper. When he founded the Appledore House on nearby Appledore Island, his daughter served as hostess, becoming famous in Boston's literary circles for her entertaining. She is known today for her writings as well as her island garden (see page 21), memorialized in watercolors by Childe Hassam.

Instead of wealthy vacationers, the island now attracts students of marine science to the Shoals Marine Laboratory, but except for the lab buildings, the island is bare, and the reason for its original name, Hog Island, is hard to miss: Its rounded stone "back" resembles a hog wallowing in brine. The ferry stops on adjacent Star Island — named by sailors for its many-pointed shape — where the horizon is dominated by the Star Island Conference Center. Reminiscent of the old Appledore House, leveled by fire in 1914, the center has long been the site of nondenominational summer conferences dedicated "to the glory of God and the . . . brotherhood of all earnest souls. . . ."

Day visitors to Star Island may explore the terrain on a

guided tour. Just to the right of the conference center, on the northwestern shore, are signs of the glacier that sculpted these ocean peaks the same way it shaped the White Mountains (see box, page 132). The granite is scraped and scarred here, marked by the ice mass as it inched along, lopping off the island summits and depositing them in chunks on the ocean floor to the southeast. Today, lobsters thrive along this rocky bottom, where they find protection and food.

Here, too, wedged between the steep walls of an eroded trap dike, is a tiny oasis that could qualify as the world's smallest sandy beach. Early settlers to these islands, once the largest supplier of fish to Europe, had to live resourcefully. To build their houses, they often had to tear apart the very ships in which they had arrived. The foundations were held together with mortar made from the sand of this minuscule beach.

The islands – especially Appledore with its pond – provide habitat for a variety of birds. Herring and black-backed gulls nest thickly on Appledore, Smuttynose, and Duck islands. Double-crested cormorants nest on Duck. Some birds, including snowy egrets and glossy ibis, fly to the salt marshes at Odiorne Point to feed during the day. And the black guillemot makes the rocky Isles of Shoals its southernmost nesting point in the Northern Hemisphere.

Leaving Star Island, the last landmark you see is the Gosport chapel, where islanders once held all-night prayer vigils for the safe return of their fishermen. Lanterns in the windows burned all through the stormy nights, turning the stone chapel into a lighthouse. Today, on summer evenings, the tradition continues. During hushed candlelight services, the chapel windows flicker with light, tiny beacons in the watery darkness.

To do: bird-watching, walking tours, and picnicking on Star Island. Contact ISSCO, Barker Wharf, 315 Market Street, Portsmouth, NH 03801; 800-894-5509 (in NH); 800-441-4620. Two other firms offer non-stopover cruises to the Isles: N.H. Seacoast

Cruises, Route 1A (P.O. Box 232), Rye, NH 03870; 800-734-6488; and Portsmouth Harbor Cruises, 64 Ceres Street, Portsmouth, NH 03801; 800-776-0915. Call for times and prices. (For information about week-long seminars available to the public, contact the Shoals Marine Laboratory, Cornell University, Ithaca, NY 14853; 607-255-3717.)

FULLER GARDENS

Walk through two sweet-scented acres of formal gardens: roses, perennials, annuals, a Japanese garden, and a conservatory of tropical and desert plants.

Directions: From State 1A in Hampton, turn left onto Willow Avenue 200 yards north of the junction of State 101D and State 1A. The gardens are on the left after a few hundred yards.

On a misty midsummer day, fine droplets of water glisten on every petal of every rosebush in Fuller Gardens. Floribundas, hybrid teas, grandifloras, miniatures, climbers — 2,000 bushes in all. Roses in shades of red, pink, white, yellow. Roses in 120 varieties. Roses whose sweet smell hangs thick in the warm, damp air. One of the few remaining estate gardens of the early twentieth century, Fuller Gardens was designed in the 1920s by the noted landscape architect Arthur Shurtleff. Additions were made in the 1930s by the famous Olmsted brothers, designers of New York's Central Park.

From the beginning, these gardens were meant to be enjoyed. A 1938 report by the Olmsted firm noted that the Fullers "took a great deal of pleasure . . . from seeing a great many people in the garden . . . enjoying it." Today's visitors can delight in two acres of perfectly groomed color, which include an All-American Rose Display Garden and All-American Award-Winning Annuals. The formal garden in front has been meticulously designed with high hedges, fountains, statues, and tiny marble pathways. Its neatly cut beds are wider at one end, creating an optical illusion. From the gate at the far end, where the Fullers used to enter, the garden appears much longer than it is. The best time to appreciate this design is in early spring, before the roses bloom, when the garden is spare and lean — all angles and patterns.

A less formal side garden has mixed beds of roses and espaliered fruit trees climbing the wall. In the back garden, visitors can see rosa mundi, one of the oldest varieties of roses. Through the giant hedge of arborvitae, completely surrounded, lies a tiny Japanese garden, cool and dark. Inside, rhododendron, wisteria, and azaleas spill color into the green; a small footbridge crosses a pond swimming with goldfish; ferns sway; and water runs softly across stones — the sound of serenity itself.

Contact Fuller Gardens, 10 Willow Avenue, North Hampton, NH 03862; 603-964-5414.

GARDENS OF THE PORTSMOUTH AREA
Portsmouth is a city of secret gardens, hidden behind hedges and fences, waiting to be discovered. Most are open from June through October and charge a small fee. Call for specific times and dates.

Moffatt-Ladd House
In the Colonial gardens behind the Moffatt-Ladd House, history, quite literally, has put down strong roots. In 1763, John Moffatt built this house as a wedding gift for his son; a damask rose brought from England by his son's bride still blooms in the garden. On the east side of the house stands a giant horse-chestnut tree planted in 1776 by William Whipple, Moffatt's son-in-law, upon his return from signing the Declaration of Independence. The four terraces or garden rooms behind this stately

Georgian mansion include a spiral trellis of old Portsmouth design, an herb garden, and a cutting garden – complete with neatly manicured grass-covered steps. *154 Market Street; 603-436-8221.*

Governor John Langdon House
The best way to appreciate the gardens behind the 1784 John Langdon House is to look up – and down. Up at the roses overhead, down at the roses on all sides. The early-twentieth-century arbor stretches 150 sweet-smelling feet, a tunnel of color and scent. When the roses become dizzying, you can enjoy the perfectly symmetrical perennial border, bursting with mirror-image plantings of peonies, Siberian iris, globe thistle, and lilies. The best time to visit and catch a bit of both shows, the roses and the perennials, is late June or early July. *Society for the Preservation of New England Antiquities (SPNEA), 143 Pleasant Street; 603-436-3205.*

Rundlet-May House
James Rundlet was a meticulous record-keeper. The grapes, roses, lilacs, and flowering shrubs he bought for his nineteenth-century garden amounted to precisely $104; the 1812 map of his garden details the layout of terraces, paths, and banks that still form the outline of this charming garden. The plantings themselves are a mix of annuals and perennials that reflect the idiosyncratic tastes of the second generation who lived here: several large square beds filled only with peonies; a garden of Solomon's seal and tiger lilies; spiral rose-covered trellises unique to Portsmouth; and a pet cemetery filled with great orange poppies. Any time you go, something will be in bloom. *SPNEA, 364 Middle Street; 603-436-3205.*

Wentworth-Coolidge Mansion
The best way to appreciate the lilacs that bloom at the Wentworth-

Coolidge Mansion is to crouch down and crawl underneath one — a week or so before Memorial Day. There's the scent, yes — an aroma so sweet it hangs in the air like a purple haze. But underneath are the trunks, thick and twisted, rough and creased, like ancient hands, beautiful with age. In fact, these lilacs came from England more than two centuries ago, the first to arrive in this country. They still bloom today, cascading masses in every corner of this little point of land by the sea. *Little Harbor Road; 603-436-6607.*

Prescott Park

At one end of Prescott Park, row after neat row of color stretches across the wide lawn to the sea: towering tithonia; brilliant magenta amaranthus (a.k.a. "Love lies bleeding"); feathery celosia; tufted beds of purple, pink, and white alyssum; petunias, pansies, and impatiens. Everything's labeled here, the common and the uncommon, in one of the few All-America display gardens in the Northeast. The park also has a formal garden with fountains and Japanese crabapple trees, a rose garden, and a vertical flower wall covered with fibrous begonias, impatiens, trailing verbena, creeping zinnia, and celosia. *Marcy Street, across from Strawbery Banke; 603-431-8748.*

Celia Thaxter's Garden

Celia Thaxter cultivated her garden on Appledore Island, in the Isles of Shoals, surrounded by the sea. In her book, *Among the Isles of Shoals,* published in 1873, she marvels at this tiny, rock-bound plot of land: "As for garden flowers," she notes, "when you plant them in this soil they fairly run mad with color. . . . The little spot of earth on which they grow at the island is like a mass of jewels. Who shall describe the pansies, richly streaked with burning gold; the dark velvet coreopsis and the nasturtiums; the larkspurs, blue and brilliant as lapis-lazuli; the 'ardent marigolds,' that flame like mimic suns? . . . Why should the poppies blaze in such imperial scarlet? What quality is hidden in this thin soil, which so transfigures all the familiar flowers with fresh beauty?" By special arrangement, Celia's gardens, carefully reconstructed by local garden clubs, can be visited today.

For reservations and price information, contact Shoals Marine Laboratory, Cornell University, Ithaca, NY 14853; 607-254-2900. (Tours are conducted only on Wednesdays, from mid-June through Labor Day.)

URBAN FORESTRY CENTER

These 170 acres of fields, forests, and salt marsh on the outskirts of Portsmouth include self-guided forest interpretive trails, a small herb garden and perennial border, and a "Garden of the Senses" that is handicapped-accessible.

Directions: From the Portsmouth traffic circle, take the US 1 bypass to US 1 South (Lafayette Road). At the stoplight near Yoken's Restaurant, turn left onto Elwyn Road and then take the first left into the center.

Red pines line the entrance to the Urban Forestry Center, stretching away from the winding road in perfect rows, a dark and shadowy retreat – green needles overhead, brown needles underfoot, nothing but silence in between. Planted as a windbreak by John Elwyn Stone, who donated this property to the state, the pines serve as a buffer from the busy city just seconds away. Today Stone's land is used as a tree farm, wildlife sanctuary, and garden demonstration site. The two-mile Brooks Trail threads first through open field and past the salt marsh, tufted in shifting shades of brown and green. Small birdhouses along the way provide nesting sites for tree swallows to help control mosquitoes.

The trail continues through woodlands – much of them

managed to demonstrate forestry principles such as pruning, thinning, and harvesting – and winds up, finally, at the edge of Sagamore Creek, a good place for bird-watchers to spot herons and other shorebirds. On overcast days, condensation clings to every surface, the air smells faintly of salt, and a distant foghorn calls repeatedly into the heavy grayness.

To do: walking, bird-watching, picnicking; landscaping ideas throughout the grounds; educational programs. Contact the New Hampshire Division of Forests and Lands – Urban Forestry Center, 45 Elwyn Road, Portsmouth, NH 03801; 603-431-6774.

EAST FOSS FARM

This multiple-use property, owned and managed by the University of New Hampshire, is a good setting for learning about the benefits of diverse habitats – and for watching for warblers (see box next page).

Directions: From US 4, follow State 155A to Mill Road in Durham Center. Drive .6 mile and turn left onto Foss Farm Road. Continue .3 mile to an unmarked dirt road on the right. Park a short distance in, by the gate.

Modified clear-cuts, prescribed burning, early spring burns versus early summer burns – on the west side of 164-acre Foss Farm you'll see the results of each of these habitat-management techniques. Clear-cutting on the edge of a wetland has improved habitat for ruffed grouse and woodcock, which need the aspen that grows in under these conditions. Prescribed burning can encourage staghorn sumac and American hazelnut, both good wildlife foods. For lots of raspberries and blackberries, burn in early spring; early summer burns produce patchy vegetation. Most of New Hampshire, like the east part of the Foss Farm property, has grown up to woods. But animals require more than woodlands. They have very specific needs, and landowners can learn to maximize the diversity of habitats on their property to encourage wildlife. Foss Farm is one of seven wildlife habitat-management trails around the state (see pages 41 and 77).

SPRING BIRDING TIP:
HEAD FOR THE WOODS – AND THE WATER

Signs of spring come early. The great horned owl starts incubating eggs as early as February. Even when the weather is still cold, you'll begin to hear the first notes of the changing season: The white-breasted nuthatch, the tufted titmouse, the chickadees all sing early. In March, the robins, bluebirds, cedar waxwings, and flickers return, followed in April by the hermit thrush, the yellow-rumped warbler, and the pine warbler. By mid-May, things are really in swing. "I consider the third week of May the most ideal time for birding," says Steve Mirick, president of the Seacoast chapter of the Audubon Society of New Hampshire.

"In spring I recommend *Foss Farm* in Durham," says Mirick, "where you'll find lots of prairie warblers and blue-winged warblers. The males, especially in spring, are like bright little jewels." He adds that Foss Farm is one of the best places in the state to look for the very rare golden-winged warbler. This tiny gem of a bird prefers wet, overgrown fields, many of which are being developed or giving way to woodlands. Its southern habitat, the rain forest, is also disappearing (see box, page 64). Foss Farm also provides habitat for pileated woodpeckers, American woodcock, and barred owls. Scarlet tanagers, ovenbirds, and wood and hermit thrushes all nest here; field sparrows and bluebirds nest in the open fields on the west end of the property.

On the waters of *Great Bay,* spring is the time for migrating waterfowl: wood ducks, thousands of Canada geese, and large flocks of scaup – as many as 4,000 of them in a flock. "You won't see this many birds all at once anywhere else in the state," says Mirick. (Great Bay's Sandy Point is the best place to look for scaup. See entry on page 5 for directions.)

For more information, contact UNH Cooperative Extension, 110 Pettee Hall, University of New Hampshire, Durham, NH 03824; 603-862-3594, or 862-1065.

BELLAMY RIVER WILDLIFE SANCTUARY

This twenty-acre piece of riverside land in Dover, another part of the Great Bay ecosystem, is a haven for wildlife and nature lovers.

Directions: From US 4 in Dover, drive 2.5 miles east of the junction with State 108. Turn onto Back River Road. After .8 mile, take Bayview Road to the right. At the end of Bayview, just past a stand of mature pines, bear left on a gravel road and continue through the field to the parking area.

Great blue and green-backed herons thrive in the tidal flats along the Bellamy River. So do greater yellowlegs and, during migration seasons, black ducks and other waterfowl. The hardwood forest that borders the river provides habitat for ruffed grouse, yellow-shafted flickers, wood thrushes, rose-breasted grosbeaks, and barred owls. Adjacent to the sanctuary, New Hampshire Fish and Game's 400-acre River Run property (hunting is permitted), recently saved from development, will extend the acreage along this waterfront. Plans to enlarge the pond here will improve the marshland habitat, and a proposed corridor between the two properties will provide a less fragmented chunk of habitat wedged into the midst of this highly developed area of the state.

To do: birding: migratory waterfowl and land birds, as well as inland wildlife; walking. Contact Audubon Society of New Hampshire, 3 Silk Farm Road, Concord, NH 03301; 603-224-9909.

BLUE JOB MOUNTAIN
The seacoast area's only mountain combines a short climb with a long view.

Directions: From Rochester, drive west on State 202A to Crown Point Road (two miles past Meaderboro Corner). Take Crown Point Road, which bears right here (202A bears left), and continue 5.5 miles past farmland and woods to a parking area on the right, just across from a farmhouse. The trail, not marked by a sign, begins on the left.

If you are on the seacoast, and you want to climb, there's only one place to go: Blue Job (1,356 feet). Unlike the biblical Job, who faced so many trials, you will find yourself untaxed by this little mountain. But if you choose the right day, clear and cloudless, you'll be amazed at how far you can see from the fire tower: north to the White Mountains, west to Vermont, south as far as Boston (with the help of binoculars), east to the Atlantic. On the way up, you'll climb through a southern hardwood forest of mostly oak, not found farther north. Plan to visit Blue Job in the fall, between September 15 and 20, for the best seat on the seacoast for hawk migration. The broad-winged hawks, which pass overhead on their way south, arrive en masse, sometimes 800 at a time.
Distance: one mile; time: forty-five minutes.

2

Monadnock Region

Once it's gone, it's gone forever.

— Motto, Friends of the Wapack

There's a movement afoot in the Monadnock region — one that began a century ago. In 1884, swift action by the Jaffrey selectmen saved Mount Monadnock from falling into the hands of a single owner. Instead, the first parcel of mountain acreage was sold to the town, and so began an active tradition of land conservation. Today, about 75,000 acres have been permanently protected — the highest concentration of local- and state-protected land anywhere in New Hampshire. More than half this land lies within five large tracts: Pisgah State Park (13,500 acres); the privately owned Andorra Forest (11,000 acres); the jointly protected "supersanctuary" (7,300 acres); the Monadnock Reservation (5,000 acres), jointly protected and owned by the Forest Society, the state, and the town of Jaffrey; and the Peirce Reservation (3,461 acres), another Forest Society holding.

And now the Greenbelt movement is under way, a regional plan for connecting major conservation areas with corridors. In addition to providing a recreational trail, the movement's goals include protection of plant and animal habitats, as well as scenic and historic preservation. And it's a team effort involving land-owners, conservation commissions, land trusts, and the state. As the Greenbelt grows, linking the region's protected areas, perhaps those who climb Monadnock in years to come, in search of an unspoiled green view, will look down and murmur, with a sigh of relief, "Once it's saved, it's saved forever."

MEETINGHOUSE POND

This fifty-acre pond is a good place for a twilight walk or an early morning paddle in a canoe or kayak.

Directions: From Keene, take State 101 east to the junction with State 124 in Marlborough. Turn south on 124 and go 2.3 miles. Then turn left on Meetinghouse Pond Road (*not* Meetinghouse Road) and drive .5 mile to the pond. (The road is not maintained in winter.)

The trail at Meetinghouse Pond twists through a hemlock forest and past sharp-edged boulders deposited by the glacier. Watch for the ancient giants: thick birches leaning long and white into the green; a double-trunk pine spreading its soft branches like a green-needled star above the forest canopy; a red oak, nearly two centuries old, its massive trunk crinkled with deep ridges. These trees stand defiant in the midst of a younger forest.

Along the Rocky Ridge Trail, just before it turns right, follow the short spur that leads to the edge of the pond. Stand quietly here, binoculars in hand, and wait. Dragonflies dart and dive across the water, their wings catching the early evening sun. Bullfrogs croak their deep-throated sawing. Scan the horizon. Suddenly, a merganser flies from the woods in a swift arc, his calling raucous in the stillness. Landing with a splash, he turns toward the nearby sphagnum mat in search of supper, his spiky brown hood cutting a punk-profile in your binocular lens.

To do: walking, canoeing, bird-watching, snowshoeing. (This property abuts a town picnic area.) Contact the Audubon Society of New Hampshire (ASNH), 3 Silk Farm Road, Concord, NH 03301; 603-224-9909.

MOUNT MONADNOCK

Considered the second most frequently climbed mountain in the world (after Japan's Mount Fuji), this National Natural Landmark is crisscrossed by forty miles of trails and capped by a wide-open summit.

Directions: From Jaffrey, take State 124 west two miles to Dublin Road and follow signs to Monadnock State Park. A small fee is collected. For directions to other trailheads, contact park headquarters (see page 30).

Nineteenth-century naturalist Henry David Thoreau loved this mountain and climbed it often. "It is remarkable," he once wrote, "what haste visitors make to get to the top of the mountain and then look away from it. . . . The great charm is not to look off from a height but to walk over this novel and wonderful rocky surface." To appreciate this well-trod peak in the way Thoreau suggests, you have to plan: Plan not to go on a beautiful fall weekend; plan not to follow the most popular trails.

One of the most scenic routes, which follows the Pumpelly Trail along the northeast ridge, is also one of the least used. If you start from the trailhead on Lake Road in Dublin, it's also the longest (4.5 miles). A shorter alternative (3.5 miles), which allows you to see more of the mountain by descending along a different route, begins at park headquarters along the busy White

Dot Trail. It veers off shortly to pick up the Cascade Link Trail and then hooks up with what one park manager calls "the best part of the Pumpelly Trail — right where it breaks out above treeline."

From here, Monadnock's summit (3,165 feet) is with you all the way, a looming presence. Mountain cranberry and mountain sandwort cling to this "novel and wonderful rocky surface," and the Sarcophagus — a giant boulder dropped by the glacier — sits high on the ridge. Along the way, watch for two small bogs, waving with tufted cotton grass, home to the tiny insectivorous sundew. The vegetation here has changed dramatically since the nineteenth century, when fierce fires, some of them set by farmers trying to rid the mountain of wolves, stripped the summit of its spruce forest. Today, all that survives in this windswept place is a community of alpine plants usually found at higher elevations.

At the summit, your boots scrape against the more erosion-resistant schist that has left Monadnock towering above its neighbors. Here, where the view stretches across parts of all six New England states, the mountain's Algonquin name seems well chosen: *M'an-adn-oc*, "the place where is a high mountain." Anchored by the 5,000-acre Monadnock Reservation, this much-loved mountain is surrounded by thousands of protected acres, secure forever from development.

Note: Most trails that leave from the Old Toll Road off State 124 are also likely to offer quieter ascents. Keep in mind that some Monadnock trails cross private land.

To do: *hiking, cross-country skiing; picnic sites; visitors center; park store; twenty-one-site year-round campground. For a trail map and more information, contact Monadnock State Park, P.O. Box 181, Jaffrey, NH 03452; 603-532-8862. The* Monadnock Guide, *published by the Forest Society, includes natural and cultural history about this famous mountain.*

A TRIO OF LITTLE MOUNTAINS

Mount Monadnock is the highest peak in the southwest corner of the state, but it's not the only one. Below are described three smaller mountains, where the views are lovely — and the blueberries plentiful.

Pitcher Mountain

Directions: From Stoddard, follow State 123 west 1.5 miles to the parking area on the right, from which the trail departs. Follow either the fire road or the trail that is part of the Monadnock-Sunapee Greenway.

It would be hard to find a shorter hike with more expansive views — and more bountiful blueberries (pick your own and pay when you leave). This trail begins along the road to the fire tower (2,153 feet) and climbs quickly. From the summit, the Andorra Forest, on which the Forest Society holds an easement, stretches out across 11,000 protected acres, the second-largest privately held easement in New England. Some 2,650 acres of this land are managed by the Harris Center and are being preserved as wilderness — protected forever from motorized vehicles, building, and logging. Mount Monadnock's distinct peak rises, unmistakable, to the south, marking one end of the Monadnock-Sunapee Greenway, which crosses Pitcher Mountain and continues northward through the forest below. *(*Note: *The family that owns the forest also owns the mountain itself. Please be respectful of their land.) Distance: .4 mile; time: thirty minutes.*

Bald Mountain
(DePierrefeu-Willard Pond Wildlife Sanctuary)

Directions: From Hancock, follow State 123 west 3.7 miles. Bear right at the first dirt road. Drive 1.6 miles, bearing left at mailboxes, to the parking area.

The first thing to do at the base of Bald Mountain is make a decision: Do you hike the mountain first or walk along Willard Pond at its base? From the summit (2,037 feet) – a short, steep climb – there are wide views of the Monadnock region; around the pond you can look for hooded mergansers, wood ducks, and common loons. Located on the Audubon Society of New Hampshire's largest sanctuary, these 1,000 acres are somehow secluded enough to promise uncrowded trails no matter which one you choose first. During late summer, bring your blueberry bucket.

Distance: depending on which route you choose, hike for fifteen minutes or two and a half hours (mountain round-trip).

Contact ASNH, 3 Silk Farm Road, Concord, NH 03301; 603-224-9909.

A handsome male hooded merganser

Gap Mountain

Directions: From Jaffrey (north side), follow State 124 6.3 miles and turn left onto Old County Road. Drive .6 mile to a right turn. The parking area is just ahead on the left, near a seeded log landing. The trail begins near the informational kiosk.

On good-weather weekends, cars crowd the parking areas near the trailheads of Mount Monadnock's most popular hiking routes. Just minutes away, smaller Gap Mountain offers an easier, uncrowded climb and a blueberry bush–covered summit (1,862 feet). The Metacomet-Monadnock Trail, better known as the "M-and-M," meanders through the woods here, part of its route between Connecticut and New Hampshire. Stone walls along the way are reminders of the pastureland that covered most of New Hampshire a century ago.

As you near the summit, the trail heads upward among exposed boulders. Scrambling across the last of them, remember to look up. You'll be face-to-face with Mount Monadnock, its sloping peak filling most of the northern horizon. Plunk yourself by the nearest blueberry bush and start picking.

Distance: one mile; time: forty-five minutes.

To do: hiking, blueberrying. Owned by the Society for the Protection of New Hampshire Forests (SPNHF) – the Forest Society – this mountain is managed cooperatively with the state. For more information and a trail map, contact Monadnock State Park, P.O. Box 181, Jaffrey, NH 03452; 603-532-8862; or SPNHF, 54 Portsmouth Street, Concord, NH 03301; 603-224-9945.

PISGAH STATE PARK

New Hampshire's largest state park includes seven ponds, four highland ridges, numerous wetlands – and a backcountry feel.

Directions: From Chesterfield, Hinsdale, and Winchester, follow highway signs to major trailheads.

Pisgah State Park is shaped like a bowl — a 13,500-acre geological bowl filled with rough, forested terrain. The place feels wild. And that's what draws people. "We planned it carefully," says Michael Walsh, longtime former manager of New Hampshire's largest state park, "to preserve the backcountry aesthetic." Instead of concentrating use in the center of the park, trails were developed around the edges. It's easy to feel alone here — especially as you work your way deeper and deeper into the center of the park.

From each of the six trailheads — all marked by information boards with maps — you can choose short, medium, or longer hikes. History enthusiasts will want to walk or drive along the Old Chesterfield Road past twenty-four historic sites described in the trail brochure. Birders interested in water birds can follow the South Woods Trail. The Snowbrook Trail winds through beautiful wetlands.

Pisgah Reservoir (a quarter-mile, uphill portage from the upper Reservoir Road parking lot) is the place to launch out into watery solitude — and the best spot for blueberries. (For those with limited mobility, forty-acre Fullam Pond is accessible along a gravel road.) Those in search of a view should hike Mount Pisgah (1,300 feet): The Connecticut River Valley spreads out to the west, the "Pisgah bowl" and Mount Monadnock to the east.

To do: hiking, mountain biking, fishing, picnicking, canoeing, kayaking, ski touring, snowmobiling. No camping. Contact Pisgah State Park, P.O. Box 242, Winchester, NH 03470; 603-239-8153.

RHODODENDRON STATE PARK

The best time to see the show at this National Natural Landmark is early to mid-July, when sixteen acres of wild rhododendron let loose their colorful blooms.

Directions: From Fitzwilliam, drive one mile west on State 119 to the park entrance.

This forest must be enchanted. Huge shrubs with large, shiny leaves tower thirty feet overhead, lining the narrow path like the walls of some monstrous maze. This giant's garden is actually the largest stand of wild rhododendron (*Rhododendron maximum*) north of the Allegheny Mountains, and one of the few places in New England where this enormous member of the heath family is naturally occurring. Unlike the hybrids in most front yards, these rhododendron bloom in July, not June, and the blossoms are less showy. But the hush within this rhododendron forest, where white blooms bright against the mass of dark green leaves, you won't find in any front yard. *(Note: The flowers tend to go in cycles; some years there are fewer blossoms and more foliage growth.)*

To do: *walking, picnicking; wildflower trail; one-mile spur trail up Little Monadnock. Contact Monadnock State Park, P.O. Box 181, Jaffrey, NH 03452; 603-532-8862.*

MILLER STATE PARK
A 1.3-mile auto road winds its way up a mountain to New Hampshire's oldest state park, an especially popular spot on clear autumn days.

Directions: The park entrance lies four miles east of Peterborough, off State 101.

You won't be alone in Miller State Park. Established in 1891, the park covers the summit of Pack Monadnock Mountain

(2,090 feet), and the road to the top leads to breathtaking vistas. Mount Monadnock and Cunningham Pond lie to the west; Crotched Mountain, Mount Kearsarge, and on a clear day, Mount Washington, can be seen to the north; the Boston skyline rises to the south. Nearby North Pack Monadnock lies just up the ridge, which serves as a flyway for migrating hawks and neotropical migrants (see entry below and boxes, pages 38 and 64).

Until the early 1900s, both these mountains – named *pack,* or "little," by the Native Americans – were covered nearly to their summits with open pastureland. Herds of cattle driven on foot from Massachusetts farms spent the summers grazing these slopes; today, however, hikers climb through mixed hardwood forests that have grown up in the fields.

Two trails leave from the parking lot at the base of Pack Monadnock, including the Wapack Trail, which runs from Mount Watatic in Ashburnham, Massachusetts, to North Pack Monadnock in Greenfield, New Hampshire. A third trail runs up the west side of the mountain from East Mountain Road.

To do: hiking, picnicking; scenic auto road; old fire tower to climb. For a trail map, contact the New Hampshire Division of Parks and Recreation, P.O. Box 856, Concord, NH 03302; 603-271-3254.

WAPACK NATIONAL WILDLIFE REFUGE

This 1,672-acre refuge, a valuable migratory bird area, covers most of North Pack Monadnock Mountain.

Directions: From Peterborough, head north on US 202. Turn right onto Sand Hill Road and drive 4.3 miles to the trailhead at the northern end of the Wapack Trail. Park on the gravel shoulder. The trail is also accessible from Miller State Park (see page 35).

"The thing I love about this trail," says David Weir, "is that you can be by yourself — and your hike is quickly rewarded with close-in views." Weir is a conservationist and founding member of Friends of the Wapack, a group dedicated to preserving the twenty-one-mile Wapack Trail, which runs from Mount Watatic in Ashburnham, Massachusetts, to North Pack Monadnock in Greenfield, New Hampshire.

It is early morning and we are climbing North Pack, the last peak crossed by the Wapack Trail and the site of the Wapack National Wildlife Refuge. The trail winds through old hemlock stands, across several streams, and through white-pine forest full of wild sarsaparilla and rhodora. Suddenly, Weir pauses: "Listen." He cocks his head to catch the call of a warbler. "They're fulfilling the purpose of this refuge," he says, "which is to provide a way station for these migratory birds — which come all the way from Central America." (See box, page 64.) Other birds that visit the refuge include tree sparrows, winter wrens, pine grosbeaks, and cedar waxwings; thrush and warbler species nest here.

Before long, the trail emerges from the woods onto open ledges and abandoned pastureland. To the east, Winn, Rose, and Lyndeborough mountains are hazy in the early morning sunshine. The long, pure notes of a white-throated sparrow lift into the air, the sound of peace itself. A few minutes more and we come to the summit, with its wide view to the west and north: Stratton Mountain and Mount Ascutney in Vermont; Mounts Cardigan, Sunapee, Kearsarge, and, of course, Monadnock in New Hampshire.

The heavily forested Contoocook River Valley spreads out below, interrupted here and there only by a red barn in an open field or a sliver of white steeple cutting through the green. Don't forget to look up. This is a popular hawk migration area, where you might spot a red-tailed hawk, spiraling upward, disappearing into the distance.

To do: *wildlife observation, hiking, cross-country skiing, snowshoeing. For a map and the* Wapack Trail Guide *(by John Flanders), contact Friends of the Wapack, P.O. Box 115, West Peterborough, NH 03468. For more information about the refuge, contact the Wapack National Wildlife Refuge, c/o Great*

WATCHING FOR HAWKS

It happens every year, sometime between September 10 and September 20. On a good day, from the top of Crotched Mountain or North Pack you might see 1,000, even 2,000, hawks. They pass overhead in "kettles" of between 50 and 200, groups of birds flying at the same elevation, a dark shimmering of countless wings.

"It's not that they're social, really," says Meade Cadot, director of the Harris Center. "It's that they've all been waiting for the same elevator." Broad-winged hawks, he explains, are looking for thermals, rising columns of air that form over big fields, lakes, rivers, parking lots. When the conditions are good, the birds catch the same "elevator," spiraling upward on these thermals, gaining height, and then continuing southward.

Hawks tend to fly along north-south rivers, following them like road maps, so mountains like Crotched and North Pack, which overlook riverbeds, are especially good watching spots. Ideally, the day should be clear and calm, so the thermals are undisturbed. If there's a breeze, it needs to be coming out of the north or northwest so it isn't working against the birds.

Hawks can be seen during spring migration, too, but in far smaller numbers; since the mortality rate among young hawks is high during the first year, fewer make the return trip northward. Mark your calendar for September, when adults and young are flying together, the days are clear, and the elevators are running.

For more information on hawk-watching, contact the Harris Center for Conservation Education, King's Highway, Hancock, NH 03449; 603-525-3394; or ASNH, 3 Silk Farm Road, Concord, NH 03301; 603-224-9909.

Meadows National Wildlife Refuge, Weir Hill Road, Sudbury, MA 01776; 508-443-4661.

SHEILING STATE FOREST

Families with children, or anyone in the mood for an easy walk, will find a self-guided forest interpretive trail, and some surprises, in this small forest, called *Sheiling* — the Scottish word for "shelter."

Directions: From State 101, turn right and head north on Old Street Road, just before entering Peterborough. The forest is on the right about two miles down — 450 yards south of the Monadnock Community Hospital.

It starts off innocently enough. There's a little open field to cross, once the backyard of Elizabeth Yates McGreal, the woman who donated this forty-five-acre property to the state. At the start of the trail stands a white mulberry tree imported from China during the silkworm culture of the 1800s — one of the few that have adapted and survived in this climate. The trail continues past 100-foot white pines, once harvested for sailing-ship masts, and then through stands of hemlock used by deer as wintering yards.

But beware — just when you think you're out for a simple walk in the woods, there they are: two story-high boulders. Actually, they used to be a single giant boulder, but over the years it was split by frost, roots, weathering. Stand between the two rough stones looming on each side, massive and immovable, and it feels as if some giant must have torn these boulders from a rocky ledge and set them here, in the middle of the woods, to confound visitors — and to awe them.

The trail guide says they were deposited by the glacier 18,000 years ago, from Mount Ascutney in Vermont. No matter how they arrived, these things are monstrous, and they have enough angles and cracks that kids – and lots of grownups, too – will simply have to climb up. (Take note, parents: Climbing up is easier than getting down.)

To do: walking, picnicking, interpretive trail, wildflower garden, educational programs. Trail map and guide available at parking area. Contact the New Hampshire Division of Forests and Lands, P.O. Box 856, Concord, NH 03302; 603-271-3456.

HEALD TRACT
This quiet pond is a prime spot for glimpsing great blue herons.

Directions: From State 101 in Wilton, go south on State 31 toward Greenville 2.5 miles and turn right onto King Brook Road. Go .9 mile and turn left. Go .1 mile and turn right onto a dirt road.

In the stillness near dusk, at the edge of Heald Pond, anything could happen. Along the path that follows the water, pine needles give gently underfoot. Water lilies bunch in green clusters, like dripped paint. Not a leaf rustles. Suddenly the water gurgles. Then a splash. You look. Look again. Nothing. All is quiet. The secret life of the pond bubbles below the surface, so you have to be quick to spot anything.

As you continue through the woods, a trail guide, written and illustrated by the Wilton Elementary School fourth-grade class of 1987–88, helps you spot haircap moss with its wiry stems and the polypody ferns growing on rocks. It reminds you to watch for great blue herons, which love to feed at the pond, here in the midst of the 340-acre Heald Tract. But to spot them, you'll have to watch and wait, quiet as the pond itself.

To do: hiking, fishing, wildlife observation. No hunting

or boating. Pick up a trail guide at the trailhead Contact the Society for the Protection of New Hampshire Forests, 54 Portsmouth Street, Concord, NH 03301; 603-224-9945.

McCABE FOREST

Here you'll learn about forest succession and wildlife management — what you can do to improve the habitat for birds and animals on your own property.

Directions: From its intersection with State 31 in Antrim, head north on US 202. Go .2 mile and turn right onto Elm Street. After 300 feet, turn right into the parking area.

On the McCabe property, stone walls and small fields spotted with clumps of bluets are reminders of the farmland that once covered most of New Hampshire. Today the trail along this protected property cuts through grassy fields and follows No-Name Brook through the woods. The Contoocook River, one of the few New England rivers that flow north, meanders lazily along the eastern side of the property, where arching silver maples hang low over the water.

As you walk, you'll discover the importance of dead trees in a forest, learn why ruffed grouse and other wildlife depend on aspen, and walk through a reseeded log landing. With the help of naturalist Ted Levin's trail guide, *Changing Hands, Changing Lands,* available at the trailhead, you will understand more about what it means to manage a forest. The day I was here, I rounded a grassy bend, surprising a ruffed grouse, which leapt, squealing and crying, from the path before me, flapping through the tall grass. I watched transfixed, as surprised as the bird.

To do: *wildlife watching; nature trail. Contact the Society for the Protection of New Hampshire Forests, 54 Portsmouth Street, Concord, NH 03301; 603-224-9945.*

HARRIS CENTER FOR CONSERVATION EDUCATION

Surrounded by thousands of acres of "supersanctuary," the Harris Center, which offers weekend programs for the public, is a good starting point for an easy mountain hike or a quiet place to stroll.

Directions: From Hancock village, drive about two miles west on State 123 to a small "Harris Center" sign on the right. Turn left here onto Hunt's Pond Road and follow it a short distance to the King's Highway. Turn left and follow the dirt road to the center.

In the garden near the entrance to the Harris Center, a wooden post bears these words, written in several languages: "May Peace Prevail on Earth." In front of the old house, now used as a center for conservation education, the view opens out across stone walls tumbling with flowers, past a wrought-iron gate, stone benches, and crumbling fountains, to a distant mountain view. It is completely quiet. In this corner of the earth, anyway, peace prevails.

The 2,000 acres surrounding the Harris Center are part of a 7,000-acre "supersanctuary," which represents a cooperative effort among the Harris Center, New Hampshire Audubon, the Forest Society, New Hampshire Fish and Game Department, the town of Hancock, and many individual landowners to preserve a large, undisturbed tract for wildlife habitat. "You always hear people talking about cluster development," says Meade Cadot, director of the center, "but we've got to think about clustering open space. This is the key to having more exotic wildlife — bobcat, fisher, bear, and moose." (See box, page 44.)

For a better look at this land, climb to the top of Skatutakee Mountain (2,002 feet). The Harriskat Trail (1.5 miles) to the summit, which begins just across from the Harris Center, was carefully laid out according to the latest topographical maps. As a result, it's probably the easiest trail to the top of a 2,000-footer

Bobcat mother and kitten

CHANGING HABITAT: BOBCATS AND LYNX

Like housecats, bobcats go in search of windowsills — open, south-facing ledges where they can soak up the sun. Found as far south as the everglades and southern California, bobcats in New Hampshire are at the northern limit of their range, and their thin fur alone does not keep them warm. The lynx, the bobcat's Canadian relative, is better adapted to cold weather. Both animals are about the same size (sixteen to thirty pounds), but the lynx has thicker fur, and its bigger paws create a snowshoe effect that helps it survive in deep snow. Both cats feed on snowshoe hare in the winter, but when the snow is deep, the bobcat has difficulty catching its prey and is prone to starvation.

There was a time when lynx, too, inhabited New Hampshire's northern forests. But except for an infrequent visitor from New Brunswick or the Adirondacks, they are no longer found here. "The National Forest is not big enough to sustain a population of Canada lynx," says White Mountain National Forest wildlife biologist John Lanier. "At one time, the northern forests of Maine, New Hampshire, and Vermont were all hooked together. Now some of the linkages have been separated by turnpikes and large population centers, so the lynx is not as free to wander; its habitat has been fragmented on a regional scale."

Nobody knows precisely how many bobcats prowl the New Hampshire forests. What we do know is that their habitat is changing. The recent rise in the coyote population has increased competition for food; as the forest grows older, the bobcat's food supply diminishes (in addition to feeding on snowshoe hare, bobcats eat grouse and deer, animals that thrive in edge communities and not in mature forests). And as the human population continues to expand, bobcats, wary of people, are driven farther and farther away.

In southwestern New Hampshire, where connected tracts of land still provide a viable habitat, signs of bobcats can be found along the ridge between Skatutakee and Thumb mountains, on Mount Monadnock's Pumpelly Trail, and on several other trailless mountains.

Note: A good place to see a bobcat is at the Science Center of New Hampshire (see page 73). For more information on bobcats or lynx, contact the Harris Center or the Science Center.

anywhere in the region. For a longer loop, follow the Thumbs Up Trail to Thumb Mountain, with its splendid view of Mount Monadnock, and then take the Thumbs Down Trail back to the Harris Center.

It is on these little mountains and throughout the thousands of other sanctuary acres that the Harris Center pursues its goal: to teach "the value of things natural, wild and free. . . ." Environmental education programs are offered to schoolchildren throughout the year. And on weekends (except in August), the public can participate in sunset hikes, hawk watches, bird walks, mushroom forays, talks about bears, lectures about forest management, and more.

To do: *walking, hiking; interpretive loop trail; environmental programs. For more information, contact the Harris Center for Conservation Education, King's Highway, Hancock, NH 03449; 603-525-3394.*

PEIRCE WILDLIFE AND FOREST RESERVATION

It's not hard to be alone in these 3,461 acres, which include more than ten miles of trails and woods roads winding through deep forest stands, around beaver ponds, and across a ledge.

Directions: From State 9 in Stoddard, go two miles west on State 123. Turn right at the fire station, cross a bridge, and immediately bear right onto a dirt road. Go one mile and park on the left. The Trout-n-Bacon Trail begins thirty yards back at a small brook.

On a cool spring day, the brown leaves of autumn still rustle underfoot along the Trout-n-Bacon Trail, but the forest floor is in bloom: hobblebush bobs under the weight of its bunched white flowers; sassafras unfurls its shiny red leaves; and painted trillium raises its rose-streaked, star-shaped petals.

Signs of moose mark the path — big hoofprints in the soft

mud, brown scat piled along the trail. Sun filters through the canopy overhead, casting mottled shadows. The trail bends, suddenly, through a dense stand of spruce, and the light dims. The forest here is dark and ominous, dead branches poking like jagged fingers from every tree trunk.

Two hours of walking bring you out of the woods onto Bacon Ledge – and a splendid view. To the west, the hills of the Monadnock Greenway stretch toward Mount Sunapee. Pitcher Mountain, capped with a fire tower, is easy to spot. Mount Kearsarge and Vermont's Mount Ascutney loom to the north. In every direction, shades of green shift in the afternoon sun. The trail register, rolled into a plastic bottle and wedged into a cairn, includes several years' worth of names and comments – visitors from Colorado, Texas, New Jersey, even England. Except for these signatures, there is no sign that anyone has come this way.

The trail continues through the woods, looping back over the Ski Trail (for those who want a shorter walk) or continuing toward the sharp turn where the trail heads back along the old logging road. Just before this intersection, the trail passes a small, shingled summer cottage once used by Elizabeth Babcock. When she gave this property to the Forest Society, she named it in honor of Charles Peirce, a local mapmaker, teacher, and hiker who loved these woods and knew them well.

With his students, Peirce mapped miles and miles of this unspoiled land. The cottage sits just above one of his favorite spots, Trout Pond. Coming upon the secluded 9.5-acre pond, the reflection of Nancy Mountain rippling slightly in the dark water, is like discovering a clear, shiny treasure that's all yours.

Note: The adjacent **Williams Family Forest** *is a good place to see old-growth hardwoods. Distance: (Trout-n-Bacon Trail) six miles. A map, and possibly a compass, are a must for this trip. Contact the Society for the Protection of New Hampshire Forests (Forest Society), 54 Portsmouth Street, Concord, NH 03301; 603-224-9945. The Forest Society's* Monadnock-

Sunapee Greenway Trail Guide *contains a map and a good description of this trail.*

MADAME SHERRI FOREST

The woods are gradually reclaiming this land, once the site of a glamorous castle and a flamboyant lifestyle.

Directions: From State 9 heading west (toward Brattleboro, Vermont), turn left onto Gulf Road just before crossing the Connecticut River. Bear left at the fork and continue approximately 2.5 miles. Park at the red SPNHF gate on the right side of Gulf Road.

An arched stone bridge, a towering chimney, a curving stairway, a crumbling foundation – these are all that remain of the colorful life of Madame Sherri, a Paris-born theatrical costume designer who once threw lavish parties for her New York friends here at Chesterfield "Castle." Today, this tumbledown stone skeleton sits in the midst of 488 acres, gradually being reclaimed by the woodland itself. Wild turkeys roam beneath the giant sugar maples that edge the foundation. Deer, moose, beaver, otter, and an occasional bear have been spotted around Indian Pond, farther along the trail. And the property once hosted a population of eastern rattlesnakes, now eradicated in New Hampshire.

As you walk, watch for "the invisible line." This property, on the eastern slope of 1,335-foot Wantastiquet Mountain, is at precisely the right latitude to include two distinct types of New England forest communities: the spruce-fir forests of the north and the temperate deciduous woods of the south (see box, next page). There are also superb views from the high, open ledges of Wantastiquet: the Connecticut River to the west, the Berkshires to the south, Mount Monadnock to the east.

To do: hiking. For a map, contact the SPNHF, 54 Portsmouth Street, Concord, NH 03301; 603-224-9945.

NEW HAMPSHIRE'S FORESTS

"The simplest way to understand New Hampshire's forests is to divide them into three zones," explains J. B. Cullen, of the New Hampshire Division of Forests and Lands. The southeastern part of the state, below a diagonal line stretching from Keene to Conway, is forested primarily with white pine. North of this line, through the White Mountain National Forest to Littleton and Berlin, the forest consists of northern hardwoods: sugar maples, beech, and yellow birch. The northern part of the state, primarily private paper-company land, is forested with red spruce and balsam fir, plus some tamarack. Spread throughout these regions, the red maple is the most prominent tree of all, making up 47 percent of the forest.

In all, New Hampshire has seventy-four native tree species: Sixty-two of them are hardwoods, which thrive in deeper, better-drained soils; twelve are softwoods, or conifers, which can survive in harsher conditions and more nutrient-poor soil and generally are found at higher elevations. The "lines" between zones, however, are always invisible—and quite jagged. In the Madame Sherri Forest, for example, which lies right on the line between zones, you can find some unusual juxtapositions of species: a spruce, usually found much farther north, growing alongside a sassafras tree, usually found much farther south.

3

Merrimack Valley

Just specimens is all New Hampshire has,
One each of everything as in a showcase. . . .
— Robert Frost, "New Hampshire"

Robert Frost's New Hampshire has changed. In the Merrimack Valley, where the poet spent some of his most productive years, pockets of green remain, including one of the state's largest parks, but mostly the green is wedged in among shopping malls and along the edges of cities. Ponemah Bog lies within shouting distance of a busy highway in Amherst. The city of Manchester, with the help of the Land Conservation Investment Program, recently salvaged one of its last stretches of undeveloped riverfront. In Concord, the federally endangered Karner blue butterfly survives on a strip of power-company land cutting across what remains of the pine barrens that once covered this area.

The Karner blue, officially adopted as the state butterfly, is on the verge of becoming merely a showcase specimen, a candidate for Frost's poem. Found nowhere else in New England, and few places worldwide, the butterfly fights for its fragile existence here among the pitch pines, feeding on the endangered blue lupine, its only food source during the larval stage of its life cycle. Just minutes from the Karner blue's threatened habitat, in their Concord offices, New Hampshire's conservation organizations continue their own fight – to save and manage other threatened habitats, to protect the state's green spaces.

PONEMAH BOG
This short boardwalk stroll leads to a three-acre pond surrounded by a floating sphagnum mat and, in mid-May, a magenta cloud of rhodora blossoms.

Directions: From State 101A in Amherst, follow Boston Post Road (across from Boston Post Plaza) to Stearns Road on the left. Take the first left onto Rhodora Drive. Continue to the trailhead and the parking area.

Walking through a bog sounds funny. Each step sinks with a squish. The narrow boardwalk here is suspended in a soggy mass of moss and foliage above what was once a deep kettlehole pond (see page 102). Sphagnum moss stretches away on both sides in a quivering floating carpet. If you time it right, you'll catch the show that has made this little bog famous: For two weeks in mid-May, magenta rhodora blossoms spread out in all directions, and bog-walkers stand waist-high in color.

But the bog is pretty any time of year. Throughout the spring, summer, and fall, bog cotton sprouts in spiky clusters against the green. In May, bright dabs of color – pink lady's slippers – dot the early part of the trail, which winds through a dry upland forest of pitch pine, assorted oaks, and sweet fern. The terrain changes suddenly as the trail reaches the edge of the bog and enters an eerie floating world. On a still, gray day, with the moss quaking gently underfoot, the air faintly sweet with blossoms, it's easy to see why this place is called *Ponemah:* The Indian word, borrowed from Longfellow's "Hiawatha," means "land of the hereafter."

The mailbox at the trailhead holds copies of the trail guide and a notebook of visitor comments: "Mushy and fun!" says one. "Saw ten turtles sunning themselves," notes another. I add my own comment as I leave: "Thank goodness for this bog." In the midst of the relentless development creeping across southern New Hampshire, this bit of land, too soggy to support a parking lot or a mall, is open only to quiet walkers in waterproof boots. (Bog enthusiasts can also visit ASNH's **Smith Pond Bog** in Hopkinton.) *Contact the Audubon Society of New Hampshire, 3 Silk Farm Road, Concord, NH 03301; 603-224-9909.*

DEERING WILDLIFE SANCTUARY

This 485-acre sanctuary includes six miles of wooded trails, a thirty-acre pond, and lots of birds.

Directions: From the intersection of US 202 and State 9 in Hillsborough, go south on State 149. Travel one mile and turn left onto Clement Hill Road. After 1.5 miles, turn right at the Audubon sign and watch for the marked parking area .4 mile up the road. (*Note: Walkers are welcome along this road, which runs through private property at the center of the sanctuary, but please respect the house and grounds and surrounding fields.*)

A field on the verge of summer shimmers with color. Baltimore orioles, bluebirds, and rose-breasted grosbeaks swoop low for insects in the open grass, weaving bright paths of flight. In the orchard, scarlet tanagers and indigo buntings sing from the tops of the apple trees. The air vibrates with trilling and calling, tiny musical waterfalls of birdsong. Birds and other wildlife thrive here in these fields and woods.

Down by the pond, beaver have left their mark — trees chiseled through near the base in perfect cylindrical cuts. Wild iris grow in purple profusion near the dam at the end of the pond, a perfect spot to pause and watch the sun slip low on the opposite shore. Just yards from the dam, as the trail emerges from the woods near the second parking area, stands a red oak not to be missed. This giant candelabra tree once grew in the middle of a field, without competition, its limbs spreading and thickening year after year. Today it is completely surrounded by smaller

Male rose-breasted grosbeak — rose, black, and white

trees, the single surviving "field tree" in the midst of a dark forest.

As you walk, watch for signs of careful wildlife management: Competitive trees and shrubs have been removed from the orchard to promote the growth of blueberries as well as hawthorn, cherry, and apple trees – all important food sources for wildlife. Around the edge of Black Fox Pond, bird boxes encourage bluebirds, great crested flycatchers, and wood ducks. The fields, buzzing with insects, are kept open as feeding areas for the bright birds that flash and dart through summer evenings.

To do: walking, bird-watching; nature trails. (Winter and spring conditions on this dirt road can make car travel difficult. Call ahead.) Contact the Audubon Society of New Hampshire, 3 Silk Farm Road, Concord, NH 03301; 603-224-9909.

FOX STATE FOREST

These 1,445 acres of forest are cut through by twenty miles of trails perfect for walking, hiking, and mountain biking.

Directions: From the center of Hillsborough, drive about two miles north on Center Road. The forest entrance is on the right.

Mountain bikers love the trails at Fox State Forest. If you had in mind a slightly slower pace, follow the boardwalk that winds through Mud Pond Bog, a glacial kettlehole (see box, page 102). Or wander through a hemlock ravine, beneath dark stands of graceful old trees. There's also a marsh, good for bird-watching, and a black-gum swamp full of what Native Americans called tupelo trees, usually found much farther south. In the timber-stand improvement areas, you can see the results of thinning: "Crop trees," ringed with blue paint, have been preserved; other trees, less straight and tall, have been cut to increase the sunlight that reaches the crowns of the remaining trees – and to improve the crop.

To do: walking, hiking, mountain biking, picnicking; educational programs; forestry museum. Contact the New Hampshire Division of Forests and Lands – Fox State Forest, P.O. Box 1175, Hillsborough, NH 03244; 603-464-3453.

ROBERT FROST FARM

Poet Robert Frost drew much of the inspiration for his work from the landscape here on this Derry farm.

Directions: From I-93, take Exit 4 and go east on State 102 to Derry. At the traffic circle, drive south on State 28 for 1.7 miles.

Robert Frost loved this land. For nine years, from 1900 to 1909, he lived at this farm, walking its woods, mending its walls, learning its contours. While much of his poetry was written later – some of it while he was in England, homesick for New Hampshire – the farm held a special significance for Frost. In a letter to a friend, he once wrote, "I might say the core of all my writing was probably the five free years I had there on the farm down the road from Derry Village. . . ."

It was here, each spring, that Frost met with his neighbor to rebuild the stone wall between their two properties, a "spring mending time" ritual that became a well-loved poem. It was here that he walked, along the small brook ("Hyla Brook"), the forest thick with lady's slippers, violets, cowslips, and ferns. It was here, too, that the four-time Pulitzer Prize winner, often remembered as a harsh man, was seen as a loving father who taught his children to climb birch trees and to love the natural world.

To do: picnicking; nature trail with guide, including excerpts from Frost's poems; house tours; video. The house is open daily in summer, weekends in spring and fall; a small fee is charged. Contact the Robert Frost Farm, P.O. Box 1075, Derry, NH 03038; 603-432-3091. Off-season, contact the New Hampshire Division of Parks and Recreation, P.O. Box 856, Concord, NH 03302; 603-271-3254.

AMOSKEAG FISHWAY

Most of the fish here don't exactly jump, but the fish ladder is interesting to see, and the giant viewing window lets you stare fish straight in the eye.

Directions: From I-293 and US 3, take Amoskeag Bridge Exit 6 in Manchester. The fishway is located next to TraveLodge. Entrance is on Fletcher Street.

The fish are coming back. It's been nearly a century since salmon and shad migrated north along the Merrimack River, fighting their way against the current, returning from the Atlantic Ocean to the streams of their birth. The legendary salmon run was an annual spring event for the Native Americans, and later for the settlers, who once lived along these shores and fished its plentiful waters. But when the great dams went up to power the mills of nineteenth-century New England, the ancient journey no longer was possible.

Today, cooperative efforts of several state and federal agencies are bringing back the fish. Fish ladders are being built at dams along the river, providing access once more to salmon spawning grounds. Three downriver ladders have been completed, including the Amoskeag; four upriver locations are still to come; and the waters are being stocked with Atlantic salmon to replenish the population. By 1994, it's expected that 500 adult salmon will return to the river; by 1999, the number should reach 1,000. The goal is a self-sustaining annual run of 3,000 adult salmon in the Merrimack River.

The concrete ladder at the Amoskeag Dam has fifty-four "steps," or foot-high waterfalls, for the fish to "climb." Actually, most of them swim, although occasionally you'll see a bigger fish jump from the water. After each step, the fish can pause in a resting pool to regain strength for the next step.

Stand at the bend where the ladder twists back on itself, watch very carefully, and you might catch a glimpse of shimmering stripes, as an alewife slips through the rushing water. Several volunteer tour guides in blue hats can answer questions about hydroelectricity, the history of the dam, and, of course, the fish.

The best way to come face-to-face with a fish is to stand inside at the "Window on the River," which overlooks one of the pools halfway up the ladder. River herring (alewives), carp, largemouth bass, brown trout, shad, and Atlantic salmon float as if suspended, their mouths downturned in dour expressions, silver light winking from their shiny skin.

Open late April through mid-June. (The best time to see fish climbing the ladder is mid- through late May.) For specific dates and times, contact the Public Service Company of New Hampshire, 1000 Elm Street, P.O. Box 330, Manchester, NH 03105; 603-634-2336 or 603-626-FISH (in season).

SILK FARM WILDLIFE SANCTUARY
and AUDUBON CENTER

Headquarters for the Audubon Society of New Hampshire, this onetime silk farm, just seconds from the highway, has a short woods loop for travelers needing to stretch car-cramped legs.

THE SURVIVORS: NEW HAMPSHIRE'S ENDANGERED SPECIES
The dwarf wedge mussel doesn't get much press. Let's face it — most people have a hard time getting interested in a shell that just

happens to be the only Atlantic Coast freshwater bivalve mollusk in North America that has two lateral teeth on the right valve but only one on the left. Still, populations of this 1.5-inch creature have declined so dramatically in recent decades that it's now federally listed as endangered. As of 1990, this mussel, once found in more than seventy locations along the East Coast, now exists in only thirteen locations in six states, including New Hampshire.

It may not be glamorous, but the dwarf wedge mussel is regarded by many as an "indicator species." Stable populations indicate good water quality and a healthy aquatic ecosystem. The New Hampshire Natural Heritage Inventory (NHNHI) program is searching for the dwarf wedge mussel, along with other endangered species. Its mission: "to identify and locate rare plants, animals, and 'exemplary natural communities.'" (See box, page 87.) NHNHI – a joint initiative between The Nature Conservancy and the New Hampshire Department of Resources and Economic Development – is part of an international network of heritage programs.

New Hampshire is home to three other federally listed endangered creatures: the bald eagle and the peregrine falcon (see boxes, pages 3 and 187), as well as the delicate Karner blue butterfly. Endangered plant species in the state include Robbins' cinquefoil, which grows above the treeline (see box, page 148); the northeastern bulrush, an obscure water reed; and Jessup's milk-vetch. Dependent on ice scouring to clear away competing vegetation, the milk-vetch grows on three ledgy outcroppings along the Connecticut River – and nowhere else in the world.

Perhaps the most famous endangered plant in New Hampshire is the small whorled pogonia, probably the rarest orchid east of the Mississippi River and north of Florida. As of 1991, eighty-six populations, of about 2,600 plants, were known to exist; New Hampshire is home to more than thirty of these populations, more than anywhere else in the world. The small whorled pogonia blooms on the forest floor, its long, greenish yellow flower dangling above a circular "whorl" of leaves. Like other orchids, it can remain dormant for years, waiting for favorable conditions, before emerging from the earth. But these days, as its habitat is lost to development, the small whorled pogonia is emerging in fewer and fewer places.

Directions: From I-93, take Exit 11 onto I-89. Then take Exit 2 and follow signs for the Audubon Center.

Sometime's nature's greatest wonders are its tiniest. On this short trail, in mid-May, patches of the forest floor turn purple — delicate, dangling, wildflower purple. The fringed polygala — more commonly, and descriptively, known as "bird-on-the-wing" — is worth a stop, even if there's no time for the short walk out to Great Turkey Pond. Along the trail, other colors, too, speckle the pine-needled floor: white starflowers, red wintergreen berries, yellow and pink eastern columbine. This is the time to marvel at the "vernal photosynthetics," flowers that bloom in the forest before the leaves come out. In a few weeks, the woods will be summer-green. Walk the trail in autumn, just before the leaves fall, and the woods will once more be filled with color.

The headquarters of the Audubon Society of New Hampshire (ASNH), located on this property, is open year-round. It is here, in what was once the old farmhouse, that the organization manages its thirty sites — covering more than 4,000 acres of protected land. The Nature Store inside sells books, bird feeders, and other treasures. And kids love climbing to the aerie at the very top of the building for a bird's-eye view of the surrounding land.

Also, be sure the kids say hello to Sage and G.P., two barred owls that live in a cage by the garage. These permanently injured birds, unable to survive in the wild, are members of the education department, meeting schoolchildren throughout the year. When they are in, they sit unmoving, blinking giant yellow eyes from their dark roosting spot.

You may want to visit two other ASNH sanctuaries in the area: The oak, maple, and birch forest at the **Chase Sanctuary** in Hopkinton is a nesting site for a dozen or so species of warblers.

A barred owl

Smith Pond Bog in Hopkinton, once a kettlehole pond, is an outdoor classroom for learning about bog habitat.

Contact Audubon Society of New Hampshire, 3 Silk Farm Road, Concord, NH 03301; 603-224-9909.

MERRIMACK RIVER OUTDOOR EDUCATION AREA and CONSERVATION CENTER

Seventy-five protected acres in the midst of Concord, New Hampshire's capital, offer a walk through the woods and along the Merrimack River, as well as a tour of a solar-heated facility, headquarters for the Society for the Protection of New Hampshire Forests (SPNHF).

Directions: From I-93 in Concord, take Exit 16 and follow the brown conservation signs.

The education begins the minute you set foot on the wooden stairway that leads down, down, down into the steep ravine and onto the floodplain. Hand-lettered signs made by a loyal Forest Society volunteer identify the white oak used for barrel staves and shipbuilding; Solomon's seal, with paired drooping yellow flowers that appear in late May; and Christmas fern, which stays green throughout the winter and grows all over the hill. Several trails cross the floodplain floor and eventually lead to the edge of the great Merrimack River, where the land falls away sharply, carved by erosion. A highway bridge spans the river at the next bend, within sight and sound. But there is something magnificent still about this river and its winding course, from which the native people took their name: *Penacook,* "People of the Crooked Place."

A giant green ash on the river's edge, felled by Hurricane Gloria in 1985, is a sobering reminder of nature's constant maneuvering. Now gray and cracked, the magnificent tree has split open to reveal hundreds of tiny rings. Just beyond the ash, an overgrown white-pine plantation has become a wildlife shelter. The trees stretch out in precise rows, so thick with dead branches below that walking is impossible — except at one end of the plantation, where the lower branches have been pruned. Here, the trunks grow as straight and true as cathedral columns, pine boughs arching overhead, silence and near-darkness below.

On the bluff above the floodplain, the Conservation Center, which houses the Forest Society, is an award-winning model of energy efficiency. About 80 percent solar-heated, the center is open for self-guided tours on weekdays from 9:00 A.M. to 4:00 P.M. and for guided tours on many winter Sundays. The Forest Society gift shop stocks "Save a Tree" tote bags, wooden games, and books such as The People Who Hugged Trees. *Pick up the* Les Clark *Nature Trail Guide at the front desk inside the building. Contact SPNHF, 54 Portsmouth Street, Concord, NH 03301; 603-224-9945.*

CHRISTA McAULIFFE PLANETARIUM

At the planetarium, you can watch the stars, visit a planet, and spin through space – any time of day, no matter what the weather.

Directions: From I-93 in Concord, take Exit 15E and follow the planetarium signs.

Night falls – several times a day – at the Christa McAuliffe Planetarium. A voice speaks from the front of the room. "How would you like to go on a trip to the surface of the moon?" Suddenly the moon, a distant four days away, begins to move closer. The stars spin past. The sound effects are eerie, like giant musical rubber bands punctuated with cymbal crashes. The moon rushes forward, and you are staring at its rough and shadowed surface while the voice explains about craters and meteors.

Settled way back in a plush, reclining seat, face tilted upward, you could almost be flat on your back in the middle of a field on a summer night – except there are no mosquitoes. And there's that voice. And you get to zip through the night sky on all sorts of galactic adventures – through exploding stars, inside a glowing spiral galaxy, across the planet Jupiter. The button box attached to your seat allows you to choose your explorations.

It all happens beneath a forty-foot dome with a complex system of computer graphics; video; a multitrack, twenty-nine-speaker sound system; forty slide projectors; special effects; and three-dimensional star fields. One of the most technologically advanced planetariums in the world, it is dedicated to America's first teacher in space, who never returned from the 1986 Space Shuttle *Challenger* mission, and who wanted kids to "reach for the stars."

Call ahead for reservations: 603-271-STAR. Contact the Christa McAuliffe Planetarium, 3 Institute Drive, Concord, NH 03301; 603-271-7827.

BEAR BROOK STATE PARK

Easily accessible from I-93, the state's largest developed park has something for just about everyone.

Directions: From Hooksett, drive five miles north on State 28 to the park, which is in Allenstown.

In thirty years at Bear Brook, park manager Jim Lane has seen only one bear. But he's seen plenty of moose and other wildlife. A big beaver lodge sits smack in the middle of Bear Hill Pond, a hillock of sticks in the midst of a watery expanse. "They're usually busy working in the evening," says Lane. Another of his favorite spots is a pine-needled lookout at the edge of the campground that borders Beaver Pond. He points across the water to a maple swamp on the opposite shore. In spring, it looks unremarkable, but in autumn the maples flame red.

There's plenty more to enjoy on Bear Brook's 10,000 acres: swimming on Catamount Pond, trails through the woods and marsh, boating on Bear Hill and Beaver ponds (no motorboats), and warmwater fishing: pickerel, white perch, and bass. Handicapped-accessible Archery Pond, for fly fishing only, is stocked with trout; so is the pond for children. Archers can practice on the only public archery ranges in the state. (A four-target range is handicapped-accessible.)

Hunting, too, is permitted in this park, but the 4,000-acre wildlife refuge east of Podunk Road is open only to bow hunting. On a rainy day, stop at the museum and learn about the history of the Civilian Conservation Corps (CCC), which was involved in natural-resource conservation efforts throughout New Hampshire from 1933 to 1942. Evidence of their work, including the museum building itself, can be seen throughout the park.

To do: hiking, canoeing (canoe rentals), fishing, mountain biking, swimming, picnicking; group shelter; eighty-tent-site campground; archery range; fitness course; forty miles of snowmobile trails; ten miles of unmanaged cross-country-skiing trails. Other attractions here are the Museum of Family Camping, the Snowmobile Museum, a nature center, and a historic meetinghouse. Contact Bear Brook State Park, RR 1, Box 507, Suncook, NH 03275; 603-485-9874.

PAWTUCKAWAY STATE PARK

A huge boulder field, three little mountains, and lakeside camping are just a few of the highlights of this 5,500-acre park.

Directions: From the junction of State 101 and State 156 in Raymond, drive 3.5 miles north on State 156 to the park entrance.

Some people come here just for the boulders. Scattered at the southeast end of Round Pond is a jumble of house-size boulders, thought to be one of the largest fields of glacial erratics in the world. Ripped from the peaks of the Pawtuckaway Range as the glacier crept southward, the boulders have been designated by New Hampshire as a Natural Area.

Of course, others come to Pawtuckaway for the fishing

(bass and pickerel) on the 800-acre lake. There's good hiking, too, along twenty-five miles of trails. The peaks of the Pawtuckaway Range — North (995 feet), Middle (845 feet), and South (885 feet) — have some fine views, especially from the fire tower on the summit of South. The park is a favorite spot for mountain bikers, and campers can pitch a tent on Horse Island, right at the water's edge. Bird-watchers come in search of blackburnian warblers — neotropical migrants that prefer larger tracts of older-growth forests (see box below) — as well as blue-gray gnatcatchers, goshawks, and turkey vultures.

To do: walking, hiking, swimming, fishing, cross-country skiing, snowmobiling, camping on 170-site campground, hunting. Contact Pawtuckaway State Park, 128 Mountain Road, Raymond, NH 03077; 603-895-3031.

NORTHWOOD MEADOWS PIONEER PARK
This fully accessible park offers a quiet escape for visitors of all ages and abilities.

Directions: From US 4 in Northwood, drive about two miles past

---

NEOTROPICAL MIGRANTS: THE INCREDIBLE JOURNEY
It happens every year, sometime near dark during the first warm nights of the spring. Thousands of miles south of New Hampshire, millions of birds begin their annual flight northward. They arrive at the Yucatan Peninsula from all over Mexico, from the Caribbean, and from Central and South America. And then, as dusk falls, they depart for the next leg of their journey — across the vast Gulf of Mexico. They fly nonstop for eighteen or twenty hours across 500 miles of ocean, making the journey without food or rest.

Thrushes, tanagers, orioles, buntings, flycatchers, vireos, hummingbirds, swallows, and warblers — their names are familiar, but their stay is short. "Our birds" arrive in May or June and prepare to leave again in August, returning for the winter to the New World tropics south of the United States. New Hampshire's Fish and Game Department estimates that at least seventy of the 180 species that regularly nest in the state are "neotropical" migrants, birds with a dual citizenship. And their homes, on both continents, are in danger.

More than half the migrants — including ovenbirds, flycatchers, warblers, and vireos — winter in mature tropical forests, which are fast disappearing. But here in the Northeast, where the forest is being carved into smaller and smaller chunks, the birds face challenges too. For many birds, fragmented forests mean more competition for food and shelter. Some songbirds nest on forest floors, and the smaller the forest, the easier it is for skunks, raccoons, cats, bluejays, and other predators to find and raid the birds' nests. Cowbirds are a special threat to the seasonal visitors. These nest predators lay their own eggs in another's nest, leaving their young to be raised by the unsuspecting songbird. The aggressive young cowbirds tend to hatch earlier and eat more. Trying to feed the invader, the mother bird may ignore her own young.

"What's happening to the rain forest is a popular topic right now," says Dartmouth biology professor Richard Holmes, "but our research points to the breeding ground as being a crucial point in the life cycle. If a species produces a large brood one year, it will affect subsequent population numbers." The largest semiprotected area in New Hampshire for birds that need unfragmented interior forests, points out Holmes, is the White Mountain National Forest, although logging occurs there, as well. At the same time, other species require open fields or partially grown-up, shrub-filled fields. Once these bushes grow too big, some shrub dwellers, like the mourning warbler, will no longer nest here and will lose their habitat.

The specific needs of these individual species bring a new complexity to conservation efforts. In the early part of the century, when birds were popular targets for hunters and collectors, a "save the birds" movement instigated the founding of the first bird sanctuaries (see entry on page 105). Today's "save the birds" movement requires a greater understanding, on an international scale, of the need for diverse habitats and undisturbed tracts of land amid the pressures of steady development.

Coe-Brown Academy to the gated park entrance on the right, near a white farmhouse. The parking area is in front of the gate.

Here is a park-in-the-making. Acquired by the state in 1991, these 600 acres are being designed as a model facility. "The idea is to make it as universally accessible as possible," says Tom Matson of New Hampshire's Division of Parks and Recreation. "It's the first one of its kind in the country, as far as we know."

Countless volunteer hours put in by the Telephone Pioneers of America have already opened a number of hiking trails, including some that are flat, wide, and gently graded for wheelchair users. Also in the works are a fully accessible fishing pier and a canoe and rowboat launching area. In an unusual partnership between the Division of Parks and Recreation and a private company, the Telephone Pioneers will continue to manage the park, which eventually will include an educational nature center.

To do: hiking, canoeing, wildlife viewing, picnicking, cross-country skiing, snowshoeing. Contact the New Hampshire Division of Parks and Recreation, P.O. Box 856, Concord, NH 03302; 603-271-3254.

4

Lakes Region

One end of Stonedam Island lies so close to the mainland you could almost, with a running start, leap the gap. In the early 1980s, plans for development nearly bridged this gap — providing easy access to an island full of waterfront condominiums. Instead, the island was salvaged by the Lakes Region Conservation Trust (LRCT), which now owns 112 unspoiled acres on Lake Winnipesaukee's largest undeveloped island. On nearby Big Squam Lake, islands and stretches of shoreline have been protected by the Squam Lakes Association (SLA), the Squam Lakes Conservation Society (SLCS), and other groups.

These two New Hampshire lakes have long been known for their beauty. The Native Americans called Big Squam

Kees-ee-hunk-nip-ee, "the goose lake in the highlands." *Winnipesaukee* has two popular translations: "the beautiful water in the highlands" and "the smile of the Great Spirit." Today, on shorelines ringed with development and largely privately owned, conservation groups have carved out islands of land, real and figurative, for protection. They have also ensured public access to the waters that have always drawn people to this region, especially in summer. On these plots of land, at least, summertime seems safe, the woods unshatterable, the lake fadeproof.

SQUAM LAKES AREA

For more information about most of the trails in this area, contact the Squam Lakes Association (SLA), P.O. Box 204, Holderness, NH 03245; 603-968-7336. Ask for the Squam Trail Guide. *Unless specified, no camping, fires, or wheeled vehicles are permitted. Please be aware that several of these trails cross private land; the owners currently allow public access and expect their property rights to be respected.*

UNSWORTH PRESERVE

Directions: From Center Harbor, drive 3.7 miles north on Bean Road and turn left on Old Harvard Road. Go .25 mile to the parking area on the left.

The Unsworth Preserve is a quiet place, much loved by birders. In the midst of these 160 acres of mixed woods and woodland swamps, a trail follows the edge of a large pond to lookout points perfect for sitting and watching: Wood ducks, black ducks, and hooded mergansers nest here in summer; great blue herons and belted kingfishers are regular feeders. From May through the fall, a dozen species of woodland warblers can be spotted here. And otter are a good bet in almost any season, according to one regular visitor.

"In spring and fall, it's the best place in this region for the ten or twelve species of waterfowl that come through," says Beverly Ridgely, longtime birder and chairman of the Unsworth Preserve Committee. During migration, the preserve vibrates with the color and sound of countless wingbeats rising and falling across the water — flocks of ring-necked ducks, buffleheads, and common goldeneyes, as well as smaller numbers of green- and blue-winged teals and common mergansers.

To do: walking, bird-watching, canoeing, picnicking. (This may be the only preserve in New Hampshire where a canoe lies beached at the water's edge for those who come, paddle in hand.) Contact the Squam Lakes Conservation Society, P.O. Box 796, Meredith, NH 03253; 603-279-1309.

CHAMBERLAIN-REYNOLDS FOREST

Directions: Access to the forest by land is along College Road in Center Harbor, about halfway between US 3 and State 25B. The forest is also accessible by boat.

There's a perfect campsite for birders here on the south end of Big Squam Lake. The low bluff, reachable only by boat, has a view of Great Island Narrows and the swamp along Heron Cove, one of the best bird-watching areas on the lake. A boardwalk through the swamp allows visitors to tread quietly through this wetland habitat, watching for great blue herons, wood and black ducks, mallards, belted kingfishers — and the loons that nest here. Late August and September, especially, are prime times to catch the "warbler waves" that pass through the forest. At the edge of this 200-acre tract, a wide, sandy beach offers Big Squam Lake's most accessible shorefront for public use.

Belted kingfishers

To do: swimming, walking, picnicking, canoeing, camping by reservation (fire permits required). This property, owned by the New England Forestry Foundation, is managed by the Squam Lakes Association (SLA). Contact SLA.

MOON and BOWMAN ISLANDS
Directions: Located in Big Squam Lake near Holderness. For a small fee, several marinas in Holderness provide parking and launching services.

Rocky points, blueberry bushes, cool forests, sandy beaches – and water on all sides. These two little boulder-rimmed islands have all this, plus several campsites. Moon Island, with an ecology trail at one end, is the largest undeveloped island on the lake; smaller and quieter Bowman Island lies just across the 300-foot channel.

To do: walking trails, swimming, boating, picnicking, fishing, camping by reservation. Contact SLA.

WEST and EAST RATTLESNAKE

Directions: From Holderness, turn east onto State 113, drive 4.9 miles, and turn right onto Pinehurst Road. Drive .9 mile, bearing left at a fork en route, and park along the side of the road just before the gate and "Pinehurst" sign. Follow signs to the Pasture Trail, which starts just up the road on the left by the old saphouse.

"If I could take someone on only one short hike in New Hampshire," says Dave Anderson, education director for the Forest Society, "I'd take them to Rattlesnake, over on Squam Lake." The view from West Rattlesnake offers everything — water, islands, mountains — and the climb is short. Hiking the Pasture Trail, instead of the heavily used Old Bridle Path (which starts from State 113), allows you to do a loop hike that begins along this shorter, steeper route to popular West Rattlesnake (1,260 feet). From here, you can cross the Ridge Trail to East Rattlesnake (1,289 feet), which is much less frequently visited.

On the way, listen for the hermit thrush, which breeds in large numbers on these slopes and fills the woods with its liquid melody during summer months. Watch, too, for several species of warblers. Just below the summit of East Rattlesnake, a colony of gnarled red pines grows stubbornly from a rocky slope. One tiny pine stands alone on the summit's ledge, a perfect spot for lunch and a view of the tranquil, island-dotted water below.

Finish your hike along the East Rattlesnake Trail back to where it meets the Pasture Trail, only .2 mile from the base.

Distance for full loop: 2.2 miles; time: eighty minutes. Contact SLA.

FIVE-FINGER POINT

Directions: The trail begins just .2 mile off the Pasture Trail up West Rattlesnake. (See directions on page 71.)

When C. Christopher Morris presented Five-Finger Point to the University of New Hampshire in 1963, he intended it "to be left undisturbed in its natural state for scientific, educational and inspirational purposes." The trail winds among white pine and oak, which grows here at the northern edge of its range. Look, too, for the broad-topped tupelo, usually found much farther south. The forest, monitored by the Squam Lakes Conservation Society (SLCS), has remained undisturbed for three decades.

On the rocky cliffs along the northwestern shore, red pine grows amid clusters of huckleberry and blueberry, which brighten to cinnamon-red in the fall. In spring, look for lady's slippers along the forest floor. In any season, you'll be walking close to the water all the way. Rocky outcrops and tiny secluded beaches give wet-feet views of Big Squam Lake, its islands, and its sun-spangled waters.

Distance to loop: .7 mile; distance around loop, 1.3 miles. **To do:** *walking, blueberrying, fishing. The point also makes a good destination for cove-loving canoeists. Contact SLCS.*

EAGLE CLIFF and RED HILL

Directions: From the traffic light in Center Harbor, go five miles north on Bean Road, just past a red farmhouse on the right. The trail begins near a large apple tree fifty feet before a yellow curve sign on the right (look for trail sign).

Edward Dane remembers climbing Red Hill as a child, past the huge Belgian workhorses that spent the summer months feasting on this hillside pasture. Today the forest has grown back on these slopes, the Lakes Region Conservation Trust holds a conservation easement on Eagle Cliff, and the Dane family continues a long tradition of sharing this hiking area with the public. The climb to Eagle Cliff will get you breathing hard, but it's short, and the view down to Big Squam Lake and across to the Sandwich Range is spectacular. If you're interested in a longer trip and still wider views, continue to the old fire tower at the summit of Red Hill (2,029 feet).

Distance from Bean Road to Eagle Cliff: .6 mile; time: thirty minutes. Distance to Red Hill from Eagle Cliff: 1.9 miles. Contact SLA.

SCIENCE CENTER OF NEW HAMPSHIRE
A 200-acre "outdoor classroom" full of live animals teaches children and adults about the natural world — and our place in it.

Directions: The Science Center is located in Holderness, at the junction of State 25 and State 113.

At the Science Center's otter exhibit, sleek furry creatures slither across rocks and splash into the pools below. Wide-eyed children clap with delight and dash down the steps for an underwater view. In the visitors center, a little boy listens, transfixed, to the recorded calls of barred owls, earphone pressed tight to his ear. In another corner of the Science Center's sanctuary, a child crouches at the edge of a shallow pool, nose-to-nose with a painted turtle.

A walk through this outdoor classroom begins at the visitors center, with a sneak preview of what you'll discover on the exhibit trail. More than a beautiful setting to observe New Hampshire wildlife, the Science Center is designed to explain four ecological principles: "adaptation, population, interrelationships, and habitat." And nobody leaves without learning more about the environment. Along the trail, kids peer among boulders and bushes to spot a red fox, bobcat, or white-tailed deer. Adults try to guess the right answers at the loon exhibit, marvel at exactly what it is that black bears eat, and discover where bats sleep.

"Up Close to Animals" programs in July and August feature naturalist-led talks and visits from live animals – bats, coyotes, reptiles, and others. The Science Center, which runs classes for schoolchildren during the year, has an ongoing goal: "to demonstrate the interdependence of all living things."

To do: exhibit trail with live animals and interpretive exhibits; live animal programs. The exhibit trail is open May 1 to October 31. Admission charged; call for times and prices. (Buildings are handicapped-accessible; the trail is partially accessible.) Contact the Science Center of New Hampshire, P.O. Box 173, Holderness, NH 03245; 603-968-7194.

WINNIPESAUKEE AREA

STONEDAM ISLAND NATURAL AREA

The largest undeveloped island in Lake Winnipesaukee has 2.5 miles of trails, environmental programs – and water's-edge views of the lake.

Directions: Weirs Beach Boat Tours offers round-trip public boat transportation to the island on weekends from Independence Day to Labor Day. The boat leaves from the Anchor Variety Store on Winnipesaukee Pier, Weirs Beach, in Laconia. Call the Lakes

Region Conservation Trust (LRCT) for cost, departure times, and parking information (see page 76). If you are in your own boat, land on the northeast side of the island near Sally's Gut.

Before exploring Stonedam Island, you may want to stop at the historic log cabin near the dock and pick up a Naturalist Knapsack. Inside you'll find the tools of a nature detective: a dipnet for scooping small creatures from the swamp, a magnifying bug box, an observation pan, directions for a scavenger hunt. The island's three trails are full of things to discover — if you know how to look.

In the hemlock grove, the pileated woodpecker has been at work, pounding out squarish holes in the tree trunks. Slender-trunked clusters of striped maple are identified by its green-and-white-lined bark and the large, three-lobed leaves that give it its other name, "goosefoot." Get a weather report from the curly black lichen or rock tripe, often called "nature's hygrometer." When the weather is humid or damp, the lichen flattens itself

Wood turtle at Stonedam Island

against the rock, showing its green side. Near the swamp, bright orange finger fungus pokes up from the forest floor in crooked little spindles.

You can explore on your own here or stop by for one of the naturalist-led programs. Learn how to read animal tracks or how to help save the songbirds. Discover the truth about animals with bad reputations. Or explore the island's swamp. "All ages get excited about what they find here," says island manager Carol Foley, who loves to help visitors learn about the many habitats on Stonedam. She scoops a salamander from the aquarium on the front porch of the cabin and explains how to examine it under a discovery scope, magnifying its tiny feet and gills and eyes. Then she picks up the resident wood turtle and shows how to count its scutes ("scoots") or rings to estimate its age. Suddenly she's talking about porcupines. "They're crepuscular creatures," she explains, "which means they're out at twilight."

The island is also home to deer as well as an occasional moose. And then there are the minks — sleek creatures that often can be spotted jumping from rock to rock along the shore.

To do: picnicking, fishing, bird-watching; self-guided nature hikes; weekend environmental education programs geared to families; weekday naturalist-led programs. Nature trail guide and map available at information board near dock. The island is open to the public on summer weekends (Saturday, 10:00 A.M.to 5:00 P.M.; Sunday, noon to 5:00 P.M.) and holidays (10:00 A.M. to 5:00 P.M.) and to members from dawn to dusk all year. Contact the Lakes Region Conservation Trust, P.O. Box 1097, Meredith, NH 03253; 603-279-7218.

FREDERICK AND PAULA ANNA MARKUS SANCTUARY

This 200-acre sanctuary on Lake Winnipesaukee includes 5,000 feet of undeveloped shoreline, as well as a loon nesting site.

Directions: Driving south on State 25, just beyond Moultonborough center, turn left onto Blake Road (at the Moultonborough Central School). Go one mile to the end and turn right onto Lees Mills Road. The Loon Center is ahead 200 yards on the left.

When New Hampshire's Loon Preservation Committee (LPC) conducted its first census in 1976, it counted only 271 loons. On Lake Winnipesaukee, there wasn't a single nesting pair. The "great northern diver," able to plummet to depths of 100 feet at speeds of up to 60 mph, was a threatened species. Today, the population has roughly doubled: In 1992, the count was 504.

At the Markus Sanctuary, site of the LPC's new headquarters, a trail winds past open meadows, through a hemlock forest, and along the water's edge, near a loon nesting site. This floating island — a man-made eight-foot-by-eight-foot cedar raft covered with snow fencing and filled with dirt and vegetation — provides safety from predators and is immune to the water fluctuation that can destroy loon nests on land. Devoted "loon rangers" across the state undertake projects like these in an on-going effort to ensure that the ancient cry of the loon will continue to echo across New Hampshire's lakes.

Pick up a trail map in the mailbox at the trailhead. Contact the LPC, Lees Mills Road (P.O. Box 604), Moultonborough, NH 03254; 603-476-LOON (5666).

KIMBALL WILDLIFE FOREST
Along this trail you'll find more than a nice view of Lake Winnipesaukee.

Directions: From Gilford, follow State 11 three miles past the Laconia Airport. The parking area is on the right side of the road.

The 280-acre Kimball Forest on Locke's Hill is designed as an outdoor classroom, full of information about wildlife habitat. Along the way, you'll discover that a dead pine tree is more than an eyesore — it could serve as a perching tree for a broad-winged hawk. The acorns dropped by red oak trees provide food for deer and grouse. The soft wood of aspen, a tree that spreads prolifically following some disturbance such as cutting or a fire, provides nesting sites for yellow-bellied sapsuckers. The two-mile trail through Kimball Forest, and its accompanying trail guide, is one of seven wildlife-habitat trails in the state maintained with assistance from the University of New Hampshire Cooperative Extension service (see entries on pages 23 and 41).

For a trail guide, contact the Gilford Town Hall, 47 Cherry Valley Road, Gilford, NH 03246; 603-524-7438; or contact the Belknap County Extension Office, P.O. Box 368, Laconia, NH 03247; 603-524-1737. (Trail guides are also available at the Gilford Library.)

BELKNAP MOUNTAIN

This mountain is a good place to survey Lake Winnipesaukee — and to ponder thousands of years of geologic history.

Directions: From Gilford village, follow State 11A to Bickford Road (1.7 miles south of the Gunstock Recreational Area road). Then turn left onto Wood Road and park near the junction. The East Gilford Trail begins to the left of the white house at the end of the road.

From the summit of Belknap Mountain (2,384 feet), most people see a splendid view — a vast lake dotted with islands, mountain ranges disappearing into the horizon. Geologists see a historical drama in progress. When the glacier melted, perhaps 14,000 years ago, it left behind a mammoth hollow in the bedrock. At the southern end of this hollow, known today as Lake Winnipesaukee, it also left huge deposits of sediment that dammed the lake, raising the water level by forty feet. Prevented from draining to the south, the lake drains instead through the Weirs and Lakeport on the west side. If you study a map, you can see how the Merrymeeting River, south of Alton, was also diverted by the sediments: It bends sharply northwest, around the dam, instead of continuing southeast toward the seacoast.

While the glacier left its indelible mark in the quartz diorite that underlies the lake, much of the surrounding land, composed of harder rock, was more resistant to erosion. Long before the glacier came through, as the earth's surface shifted and churned, molten rock bubbled up from below. In places, the earth's crust caved in on itself in nearly perfect circles, and molten rock intruded into the circular cracks, creating ring dikes of igneous rock. One of New Hampshire's lesser-known claims to fame is that it has more ring dikes than almost anywhere else in the world except Nigeria, Norway, and Sweden.

The Ossipee Mountains, visible to the west from Belknap Mountain, form a nearly perfect ring dike. Rattlesnake and Diamond islands in the lake below are part of a partially eroded dike that runs beneath the water's surface. And Belknap itself, as well as nearby Mount Major, are also part of a ring dike, geological formations with splendid views.

Distance to summit: 2.1 miles; time: 100 minutes.

KNIGHT'S POND

Herons – and kids – love to fish on this quiet, thirty-one-acre pond, surrounded by 307 protected acres.

Directions: From the traffic circle at the junctions of State 28 and State 11 in Alton, go 7.5 miles north on State 28 and turn right on Rines Road. Go 1.1 miles, bear left at the fork, and continue for

.5 mile. Turn left at the "Conservation Area" sign and drive to the parking area. The pond and trailhead are .4 mile down the dirt road. (Carry boats along this stretch to the water.) In winter and mud season, park at the sign and walk .9 mile down the woods road to the pond.

"Everyone focuses on the pond here," says Doug Smithwood, an ecologist who leads walks around Knight's Pond, "but there's a lot more to learn on the way down." He stoops to scoop sand from the sandpit at the base of Rines Hill, near the parking lot. "We are standing on glacial outwash," he explains, "the sandy deposit left behind by the melting glacier." This acrid soil is home only to trees such as pines, poplar, and birch, which can live in this harsh environment. The sweet fern that thrives here makes its own nitrogen.

To the northeast, high above the trees, is another sign of the glacier: the exposed rock of Longstack precipice, where the glacier plucked rocks from the face of the mountain as it crept south. As you head for the pond, you are treading on glacial till, rockier soil dropped by the ice as it retreated. The vegetation changes here, as pines and sweet ferns are replaced by hardwoods and other moisture-loving flora.

There's plenty more to see around the pond and marsh. In the morning, beaver are at work. Water striders lift their thread-thin legs high as they skitter across the water's surface. Back swimmers, sometimes called boatmen, propel themselves with legs that move in a rowing motion. Dragonflies swoop and dart. Like many insects, they lay their eggs below the water's surface, landing on plants and pulling themselves under. Beneath the surface swim plenty of small- and largemouth bass. Somewhere in the woods sounds the fluid many-noted song of the winter wren, a solo performance in the midsummer forest.

At the marsh, a great blue heron stands near the water's edge, solitary and gaunt. Its neck arches in a gray question mark, nearly invisible against the wooded backdrop. When it lifts, suddenly, into the air, flapping giant wings, it moves as if in slow motion, heading for a perch among the dead marsh trees. Then, just as suddenly, it vanishes, invisible again.

To do: walking, bird-watching, wildflower identification, fishing, hunting; guided nature walks on some summer weekends. (Trail guides available at the parking area.) Open 4:00 A.M. to 10:00 P.M. Contact Wolfeboro Chapter, Lakes Region Conservation Trust, P.O. Box 2235, Wolfeboro, NH 03894; 603-569-5566; or contact LRCT, P.O. Box 1097, Meredith, NH 03253; 603-279-7278.

LAKES REGION EAST

HOYT WILDLIFE SANCTUARY

A glacial esker is the best route through this woodsy sanctuary.

Directions: From the junction of State 25 and State 153 in Effingham Falls, go north (toward Conway) on State 153 for 5.3 miles to the junction with Horseleg Hill Road. The trailhead and parking are at the sanctuary sign just to the left of Horseleg Hill Road.

There's something different about this trail through the woods — something to do with perspective. It dawns on you slowly. Instead of running level along the forest floor, the trail winds along a ridge that falls away steeply on either side. The Esker Trail, which begins among the cabins at the southeast corner of Purity Lake, follows a curving glacial formation known in New England as a "horseback" or "whaleback" (see box, page 83).

Listen as you go for the black-throated blue warbler's husky song; the eastern wood pewee's plaintive whistle; the loud,

A pileated woodpecker brings home a snack

THE SCULPTED LAND: ESKERS AND KETTLEHOLES

The Lakes region is full of glacial footprints. Lake Winnipesaukee itself is the largest remnant of the continental ice sheet that once covered this area. The lakes and bogs to the east, including White Lake and Silver Lake, were created by a different sort of ice. As the glacier retreated, the power of water flowing off the melting ice spread coarse, sandy soil in its wake. Chunks of ice left behind melted slowly into the sandy soil, creating "kettles." The two small bogs near White Lake are also kettleholes, filled in to form a bog (see box, page 102). Between them runs an esker.

Once the site of a stream that tunneled beneath a melting glacier, an esker is actually a twisting pile of sand and gravel that filled the stream's tunnel. These ten- to 100-foot-high ridges served as high, dry pathways for Native Americans and early settlers. Today, many of our roads follow the backs of eskers. The Frank Bolles Nature Reserve (see page 84) is also the site of a kettlehole pond and a couple of eskers. In addition, some of the most dramatic glacial sculpture in New Hampshire can be seen in the cirques and sheep's backs of the White Mountains.

irregular cry of the pileated woodpecker. Where the path twists by the swampy areas, pause and sit with your binoculars. You have a stadiumlike view into a wildlife-rich wetland. If you're a patient spectator, you may see a great blue heron lifting like a giant shadow from its grassy hiding spot. *Contact Audubon Society of New Hampshire, 3 Silk Farm Road, Concord, NH 03301; 603-224-9909.*

THOMPSON BIRD SANCTUARY AND WILDLIFE REFUGE

This partially wheelchair-accessible sanctuary, surrounded on all sides by mountains, is superb for bird-watching.

Directions: On State 25, go to the junction with State 113, located 1.2 miles west of South Tamworth. Turn north on State 113, heading toward North Sandwich. Look for the "Audubon Society of New Hampshire" sanctuary sign on the left after 2.9 miles.

The trail begins along a shaded dirt road, and then, suddenly, the woodland gives way to a broad marshland – a perfect vantage point for bird-watching, both for walkers and wheelchair users. Pause here and watch for gypsy crossbills, kingfishers, kingbirds, red-winged blackbirds, northern waterthrush, hawks, and other birds that thrive here. The trail continues, narrow and damp, until it reaches a tiny bridge, smack in the middle of this vast, grassy wetland. On either end – the Ossipee Mountains to the southeast, the Sandwich Range to the northwest – mountains rise hazy and blue in the hot summer sun. Water gurgles beneath your feet and a warm wind blows, just barely, across the open marsh.

A century ago, the farmer who owned this land – once a hayfield – worked each day in the shadow of these mountains. Today, thanks to the work of beaver, his hayfield has become a giant wetland. On the other side of the marsh, the trail disappears into a cool hemlock woods, and signs of moose are everywhere. As you follow the deep hoofprints in the soft mud, eyes to the ground, it's hard not to feel as if moose eyes were watching you from some hidden spot in the woods.

To do: bird-watching, moose – and other wildlife – spotting; nature trail. Pick up a trail guide at the trailhead. Contact ASNH, 3 Silk Farm Road, Concord, NH 03301; 603-224-9909.

FRANK BOLLES NATURE RESERVE

This secluded woods loop, at the foot of Mount Chocorua, is rich with wildlife and glacial remains.

Directions: From Chocorua Village, follow State 16 north to Fowler's Mill Road, which bears left at the south end of Chocorua Lake. Follow Fowler's Mill Road, bearing right at the first fork, for one mile to a "Dead End" sign on a tree on the right. (Fowler's Mill Road bears left.) Follow this "dead end" road .2 mile to the small parking area.

On a quiet, late-summer day, as you enter the Bolles Reserve, you might see a broad-winged hawk lift from the trees just ahead, clearing the canopy and slipping out of sight. This hardwood forest is also inhabited by bear, moose, deer, red fox, weasel, otter — the same wildlife that naturalist Frank Bolles himself used to come here to study nearly a century ago. Much of the trail follows an old road, wide and flat, once a popular route between neighbors who lived on either side of these woods.

Long before this area was inhabited at all, the glacier passed through, sculpting the land into ridges and bowls (see box, page 83). At the south end of the Old Mail Road, the trail curves along the spine of an S-curved esker. Heron Pond, on the east side of the preserve, appeared when a chunk of glacial ice melted, filling the depression left by its own weight. Today the water level in this eight-acre "kettlehole" pond fluctuates dramatically — for reasons no one can explain. When the water is low, you can make your way across dry ground to the little blueberry-covered island. On your way down from Bickford Heights (1,080 feet), the highest point in the reserve, look for another sign of the glacier: four giant glacial erratics, solemn and gray in the middle of the woods.

To do: *walking, wildlife viewing, canoeing and swimming on Chocorua Lake, cross-country skiing, snowshoeing. This property is owned by The Nature Conservancy (TNC) and managed, along with seven other nearby parcels of land, by the Chocorua Lake Conservation Foundation (CLCF). Contact the*

*CLCF, Chocorua, NH 03817; or contact TNC, 2½ Beacon
Street, Suite 6, Concord NH 03301; 603-224-5853.*

WHITE LAKE STATE PARK

A lakeside walk with mountain views and a quiet pitch-pine
forest with two tiny bogs make this state park a fine destination in
any season.

Directions: The park entrance is just off State 16 in Tamworth.
The trail begins at the swimming beach, heading left past the boat
launch and around the lake.

Strolling around the clear waters of White Lake is like cir-
cumnavigating a large mirror. At each bend, the reflection shifts,
every view framed among leaning trunks and bending pine
boughs. From the start of the trail, at the sandy beach at the west
end of the lake, the jagged peaks of the Sandwich Range –
Whiteface, Passaconaway, Paugus, and Chocorua – rise against
the sky. The flat, pine-needled path follows close to the water all
the way, well shaded beneath white, red, and pitch pines.

After half a mile, a loop winds to the left past two small
kettlehole bogs (see page 102) in the Black Spruce Ponds Preserve (owned by the town of Tamworth). The trail continues
through a seventy-two-acre grove of pitch pine – a National
Natural Landmark that is part of the same natural community that
formed the West Branch Pine Barrens (see page 88) – and then
returns to the water's edge.

Once you finish your loop, you may want to continue your
explorations with a trip to the **Madison Boulder** (off State 113,
two miles north of Madison, about thirty minutes from the park).
One of the largest glacial erratics in the world, this monstrous
rock sits alone in the woods – all 4,662 tons of it. Geologists

have matched its rock type with the rock in White Ledge, two or three miles away. Torn from the cliff by the glacier, the boulder moved with the ice, probably about 100 feet a year, until it came to rest here. Its broad, smooth surface — three stories high, eighty-seven feet long, and twenty-three feet wide — has proved irresistible to graffiti artists. Still, it's worth a visit.

Distance around White Lake: 2.5-mile flat loop. **To do:** *walking, swimming, canoeing, birding, picnicking, camping, fishing, cross-country skiing. Two other nearby areas of interest:* **Heath Pond Bog** *(south of State 25 between Ossipee and Freedom) and the* **West Branch Pine Barrens** *(see page 88). Contact White Lake State Park, P.O. Box 273, West Ossipee, NH 03890; 603-323-7350.*

PRESERVING THE PITCH PINES: A FIERY DILEMMA

The pitch-pine forest at White Lake State Park is a prime example of the dilemma involved in preserving a pitch-pine community: Because these pitch pines have been "protected" and allowed to grow quite large, undisturbed by fire, the forest is gradually filling in with gray birch and white pine. Without fire, pitch-pine barrens eventually disappear.

At the West Branch Pine Barrens (see page 88), another pitch-pine community, the last large fire raged through in 1947. Some of the rare moths and butterflies that live among these trees can survive fire if they are in the pupal stage, burrowed a couple of inches into the soil. But many of these delicate-winged adults are destroyed by the very fire that their environment needs for survival. Thus the importance of preserving large tracts of pitch pine: If controlled burning takes place in one area of a large preserve, the creatures in the unburned area can survive. The smaller the preserved area, the more difficult it is to balance the need for burning and the need for untouched habitat.

WEST BRANCH PINE BARRENS

This short walk, through one of the best remaining examples of undisturbed pitch-pine/scrub-oak barrens in North America, is an easy side trip from White Lake State Park.

Directions: From State 16 in West Ossipee, follow State 41 (Plains Road) 1.7 miles. Just past Lily Pond on the right, look for a dirt road marked by a small "Nature Conservancy" sign. The road is just opposite the "Carved in Bark" development sign on the left. Park here and follow the dirt road to the end, where it meets the West Branch River.

Along the dirt road that runs through the West Branch Pine Barrens, pitch pines grow like crooked giants, tall and twisted, rounded cones clinging to sharp-needled branches. These trees are tough. They grow in dry, "barren" soil and they thrive on fire. Their serotinous cones, which stay tightly closed for long periods of time — sometimes years — require the tremendous heat of a forest fire before they open and release their seeds. When a fire sweeps through, consuming every branch, pitch pines sprout new shoots directly from their trunks. Even if there is nothing left but a stump, the tree will often revive.

The understory in these woods is filled mostly with scrub oak, another stump-sprouter adapted to fire and to dry, nutrient-poor soil. There are also lots of low-bush blueberry, bog laurel, and other heath plants mixed with bracken fern and sweet fern. In the spring, trailing arbutus sprinkles the forest floor with tiny pink blossoms. But most of the drama of this place is hidden. "You'd never know it from looking at it," says Nature Conservancy naturalist Patrick McCarthy, "but these pine barrens are home to thirteen rare species of night-flying moths that can live only in this environment, including the *Lithophane lepida lepida,* an owlet moth found nowhere else in New Hampshire."

A walk through these 341 acres takes you into one of the

two remaining relatively undisturbed natural communities of pitch pine in the state — and one of the best remaining examples of pitch-pine/scrub-oak barrens in North America. "We're standing in a sea of conifers in an area of mixed forests," says Mc-Carthy, pulling out a topographical map. His finger traces the outline of a large, flat area surrounded by mountains, a wide deposit of sandy glacial sediment known as an outwash fan. While pitch pines are scattered throughout the low-lying sand plains of central New Hampshire, especially in the Concord area, most of this natural community, because of its flat, well-drained soil, is a prime target for development — and much of it has been permanently paved over and built up.

To do: *short walk, cross-country skiing. For more information and a map, contact The Nature Conservancy, 2½ Beacon Street, Suite 6, Concord, NH 03301; 603-224-5853.*

5

Dartmouth–Lake Sunapee Region

There are occasions when you can hear
the mysterious language of the Earth, in water,
or coming through the trees, emanating from the
mosses, seeping through the undercurrents
of the soil, but you have to be willing
to wait and receive.

— John Hay, *The Immortal Wilderness*

When John Milton Hay built his estate on the shores of Lake Sunapee in 1891, he became part of a movement to rescue an ailing state. Hard as it is to imagine, there was a time, only a century ago, when New Hampshire was in danger of becoming a sort of "ghost state." In the years following the Civil War, people were walking off their farms, heading west for less rocky soil or to the cities, where they could make a better living. The "New Hampshire Farms for Summer Homes" program, designed to lure people back to the Granite State, encouraged the purchase of abandoned farms. It worked. Soon everyone was proclaiming the healthful and curative powers of the New Hampshire landscape. "I have nowhere found a more beautiful spot," announced Hay of his Newbury home.

And so, in a roundabout way, the conservation movement was born. The Hay estate, the Weeks estate on Mount Prospect, and The Rocks in Bethlehem — all still stand on some of the very land, now preserved, that first attracted their builders to the state (see pages 91, 167, and 168). In 1895, wealthy landowners on Lake Sunapee, including John Hay, sued the Sunapee Dam Corporation to prevent the dramatic water fluctuation that damaged their property and ruined the shoreline. Today, the Lake Sunapee Protective Association continues efforts to safeguard the lake. And New Hampshire, far from abandoned, continues the conservation movement that began a century ago.

JOHN HAY NATIONAL WILDLIFE REFUGE
The grounds of this once-private estate include an ecology trail through the woods, hillside glimpses of Lake Sunapee, and habitat for wildlife.

Directions: From Newbury, follow State 103A for 2.5 miles. Turn left at the sign into the parking area and walk along the short gravel road from there.

The gravel drive that leads to the Hay estate bends through the forest, beneath branches spreading close overhead. The house itself is set against the contours of the land, as if in an effort to coexist with, instead of dominate, its surroundings. For three generations, this property was home to the Hay family, who left a legacy of love and stewardship of the land. Now the Forest Society manages 675 acres for forestry, wildlife habitat, education, and recreation; the U.S. Fish and Wildlife Service

manages the remaining 163 acres, including one mile of shoreline along Lake Sunapee, as a migratory bird and wildlife refuge.

Near the house, visitors can stand beneath the thick and
twisted limbs of two 200-year-old sugar maples – the same ones
visible in an 1891 photograph taken shortly after John Milton
Hay had begun to purchase and preserve the surrounding farmland. He named his summer estate "The Fells," after the highlands of his ancestral Scotland. When his son Clarence inherited
the property in 1906, he and, later, his wife, Alice, began exten-
sive renovations of the house and grounds. Thanks to their
efforts, fountains, gates, walled terraces, and, most notably, a
carefully cultivated alpine garden (see box, page 94), remain for
others to enjoy.

Nature writer John Hay, son of Clarence and grandson of
John Milton Hay, remembers childhood summers spent at The
Fells, summers that instilled in him a love of the natural world.
"It is an unfortunate man or woman who has never loved a tree,"
writes Hay in his book *The Immortal Wilderness*. And he recalls
one tree in particular: "There was a white pine of fair height
standing on a knoll over a little ravine that cut the hillside slopes
above the lake, an area where my father had introduced many
species of rock plants between the granite boulders. It was in that
tree that I built a platform from which to view the world along
with the red squirrels. I inhaled its resinous scent. The wind blew
through the branches, sounding like the sea, and what distant
worlds I imagined there I can no longer remember. . . ."

Hay's books, and others, are available in the library at The
Fells, which has been restored for use as a Land Studies Center,
where educational programs help students, visitors, and local
residents explore the possibilities of coexistence with the land.
The easiest way to understand this land, though, is to step outside: Climb to the open ledges of Sunset Hill overlooking Lake
Sunapee. Wander the self-guided ecology trail. Stroll through a

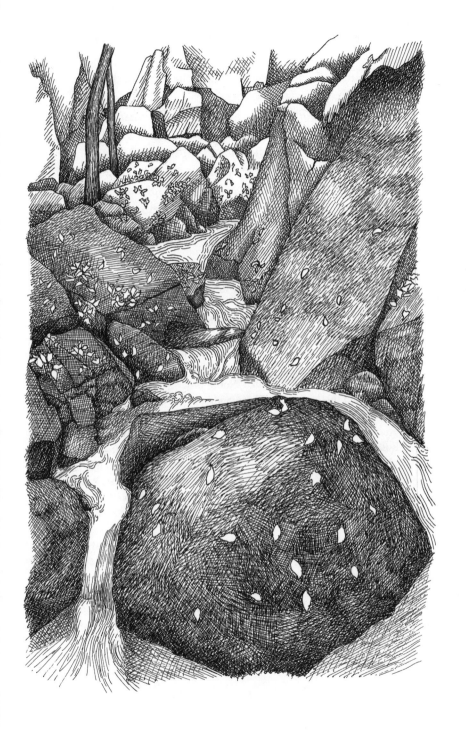

walled garden. Listen, as you go, for the wind in the branches, "sounding like the sea."

To do: walking trails, gardens, short hillside hike. The house is open weekends and holidays from late May through Columbus Day. Contact the New Hampshire Division of Parks and Recreation, P.O. Box 856, Concord, NH 03302; 603-271-3254; or the Newbury office of the Society for the Protection of New Hampshire Forests, P.O. Box 325, Newbury, NH 03255; 603-763-5958.

THE GARDENS AT THE HAY ESTATE

To some, the entrance to the Hay estate may look like an unremarkable driveway, but it's actually a finely sculpted, well-designed quarter mile that twists and turns with the land, bending around the older trees. "Everything about it seems natural," explains gardener Bill Noble, "but this is a very conscious piece of work." The driveway and naturalized plantings that surround it are indicative of the Hay family philosophy, which Noble describes as "in synch with nature and the New Hampshire landscape."

Near the house, a distinctive pebble court, perennial gardens, and a rose terrace reflect the more formal vision of Alice Hay; her husband, Clarence, expressed his aesthetic with a rock garden, complete with a bubbling brook. In his garden, which he began in 1929, he planted, at one time or another, more than 400 species. And he kept careful records. "It's very rare to find a garden like this," says Noble, "still maintained after fifty years according to an original plan."

As you explore the gardens and walk the woods trails that wind through this landscape, you'll eventually discover the Old Garden, hidden behind high stone walls, a secret room in the woods. Inside, the "room" is filled with masses of rhododendrons and a mixture of native and exotic plants, including *Cornus kousa*, Chinese dogwood; *Abies concolor*, white fir; and *Azalea kaempferi*, Japanese torch azalea. Stonework and carefully crafted design are everywhere, but there is a naturalness here, too, a sense of a place gone wild with time.

STONEY BROOK WILDLIFE SANCTUARY
Not far from the Hay estate, this 362-acre sanctuary is a good place to watch – and listen – for the pileated woodpecker.

Directions: From State 103 in Newbury, follow State 103A north three miles and turn right onto Chalk Pond Road. Trails to the two parcels begin on the left, 1.3 miles and two miles down this road.

You can choose here between a short marshland walk or a longer hike through a hardwood forest. As you go, watch for signs of the red-crested pileated woodpecker, more often heard than seen. Also known as the "logcock," it leaves a telltale trace: long, rectangular holes drilled into "snag" trees. These standing dead trees are full of delectable ants and termites, sustenance for many species of woodpeckers. The yellow-bellied sapsucker drills in another distinct pattern: a series of tiny horizontal holes. You might also notice different marks in the smooth-barked beech trees along the way – four- or five-inch scratch marks. Bears climb these trees in search of nuts, often leaving a mass of twisted branches behind after their feasts.
Contact Audubon Society of New Hampshire, 3 Silk Farm Road, Concord, NH 03301; 603-224-9909.

PILLSBURY STATE PARK
Stillwater canoeists and wildlife watchers love this undeveloped state park near the northern end of the Monadnock-Sunapee Greenway.

Directions: From Washington, drive 3.5 miles north on State 31 to the park.

Pillsbury State Park is a wild place. Its 5,000 acres provide

habitat for bear, moose, deer, fisher, and otter. Its nine ponds
and surrounding marsh and bog are home to great blue herons,
harriers, and osprey. Its forests are filled with songbirds, including redstarts, ovenbirds, Philadelphia vireos, pine warblers, and
other warbler species. "People who come here want to hear the
loons and the coyotes," says park manager Michael Morrison.
They also want to canoe, mountain bike, fish – and camp on
some of the park's unusually remote campsites. The park even
has several canoe-in sites where campers essentially have a pond
or lake to themselves.

One favorite hiking loop (about 5.5 miles) follows the Mad
Road Trail to Bacon Pond and then continues along a short con-
nector to the Monadnock-Sunapee Greenway Trail, looping back
down the Bear Pond Trail. "We've had five bear sightings on this
loop just this summer," says Morrison. Another route follows the
Pamac Trail to the Greenway Trail up to Lucia's Lookout, a
ledgy promontory that offers long-distance views south toward
Mount Monadnock and Temple and Crotched mountains. Back at
the campsite, after a day of hiking or canoeing – or both – there
is only solitude.

To do: *wildlife viewing, primitive camping, hiking, canoeing, biking, fishing, cross-country skiing, snowshoeing, ice fishing, snowmobiling. Contact Pillsbury State Park, Washington,
NH 03280; 603-863-2860.*

MOUNT SUNAPEE STATE PARK
Better known as a busy ski area, Mount Sunapee also has beautiful views and a secret mountain lake.

Directions: The park is off State 103 in Newbury, at the northern
end of Lake Sunapee.

People who love it call Mount Sunapee one of New

Keep your eyes open for black bear, but keep your distance

Hampshire's best-kept secrets: three mountain peaks, a small lake, many brooks, a sandy beachfront on Lake Sunapee – and 2,700 acres. The chairlift, base lodge, and vast macadam parking lot may not appeal to those who prefer less civilization, but the view from Mount Sunapee's summit (2,743 feet) is spectacular – rolling, green hills and mountains folding over on themselves, disappearing into the horizon. And there are plenty of ways to escape the crowds.

The Solitude Trail, which leads to White Ledges (one mile), overlooking Lake Solitude, is the one absolute "must" on the mountain. "I grew up around here," says one hiker, "and it's always been my favorite spot." A pleasant loop follows the Solitude Trail from the summit, picks up the Newbury Trail at White Ledges, and follows the Rim Trail (about 1.5 miles total) back to

---

MONADNOCK–SUNAPEE GREENWAY (MSG)

Appalachian Mountain Club (AMC) President Allen Chamberlain suggested the idea in 1919. The Society for the Protection of New Hampshire Forests (SPNHF) laid out the trail in 1921. Today, the Monadnock–Sunapee Greenway extends for forty-nine miles, linking Mount Monadnock in Jaffrey with Mount Sunapee in Newbury. More than eighty landowners voluntarily host parts of the Greenway corridor on their land. Taken together, these individual pieces of the Greenway amount to far more than a hiking trail.

The Greenway is a concept that supporters hope will serve as a catalyst to provide permanent protection of the surrounding lands. It is hoped, too, that some day Allen Chamberlain's vision of extending the Greenway will be realized – north to Mount Kearsarge and Ragged Mountain, and perhaps, eventually, to Mount Cardigan and to Mount Moosilaukee in the White Mountains, creating a "forever green, great circle around Lake Sunapee." *For more information or a* Monadnock–Sunapee Greenway Trail Guide *with a map and trail descriptions, contact SPNHF, 54 Portsmouth Street, Concord, NH 03301; 603-224-9945.*

---

the parking lot. Those interested in a longer, more challenging hike might tackle the northern end of the Monadnock–Sunapee Greenway (see box, facing page), which starts at the summit of Sunapee and heads south into Pillsbury State Park (about four miles). Hikers should be sure to have a copy of the *Monadnock–Sunapee Greenway Trail Guide.*

To do: hiking, swimming, boating (launching ramp), fishing, alpine skiing; scenic chairlift rides. No snowmobiling or cross-country skiing. For a map and more information, contact Mount Sunapee State Park, Newbury, NH 03255; 603-763-2356 (weekdays). For a Monadnock–Sunapee Greenway Trail Guide, contact the Society for the Protection of New Hampshire Forests (SPNHF), 54 Portsmouth Street, Concord, NH 03301; 603-224-9945.

MOUNT KEARSARGE

This 2,937-foot mountain is accessible from both Winslow State Park in Wilmot and from Rollins State Park in Warner. Scenic auto roads lead most of the way to the summit on both sides.

Directions: Winslow State Park is three miles south of Wilmot Flat, off State 11. Rollins State Park is four miles north of Warner, off State 103.

From Rollins State Park, the trail up Mount Kearsarge begins at the picnic area, in the midst of a grove of brilliant white birches. The rocky trail winds steadily upward, through a dark red-spruce forest. Cedar waxwings, wood thrushes, and hermit thrushes call from the branches. At the summit, the trail breaks open across expanses of naked rock covered with glacial striations, distinctive scrape marks left behind by the glacier.

Fire warden John Hill spends his days up here in the metal fire tower, scanning the surrounding hills and chatting with any hikers who stop by. He can answer questions about the weather and the wildlife up here, and he can point out the visible peaks: Mount Monadnock, 38.2 miles; Killington, 51.6 miles; Mount Washington 62.7 miles. The view seems endless in all directions. On windy days, the metal tower creaks and sways with each gust, straining against its foundation, and hawks ride the currents, circling the tower at eye level.

To do: hiking, picnicking; scenic drive. Distance: from parking lot at Winslow State Park, 1.1 miles; time: one hour; from Rollins State Park, .6 mile; time: twenty-five minutes. Contact Winslow State Park, c/o Wadleigh State Park, Kezar Lake, North Sutton, NH 03260; 603-526-6168 (Winslow); 603-456-3808 (Rollins).

PHILBRICK-CRICENTI BOG

Pitcher plants and other bog species flourish in this tundralike environment, which is easily enjoyed along a well-maintained boardwalk.

Directions: From New London, head out of town on Newport Road toward I-89 and watch for a wide shoulder area, about .5 mile past Cricenti's market. The trail starts here. From I-89, drive about 1.5 miles toward town on Newport Road. (The sign is hidden in the woods.)

There's drama underfoot at the Philbrick-Cricenti Bog. The sign at the trailhead is the first clue: "Where you now stand was once the shore of a lake. . . . Learn the story of its ongoing change by using the guide sheet as you walk the path." Guide in hand, make your way along a gravel walk, waist-high in ferns, the light overhead bright green, almost tropical. As the trail nears the bog, royal ferns and red maples give way to cinnamon ferns and, eventually, to black spruce, which thrive in water-logged, peaty soils high in acidity.

When the woods open, suddenly, to brilliant sunshine, the ground beneath your feet gives gently, each footstep sinking slightly. The boardwalk trail is set into a floating mat of sphagnum moss and grasslike sedge. Only inches below, there is nothing but stagnant water. But here above, the tundralike landscape is filled with color – and unusual plants that thrive only in bogs (see box, page 102). Labrador tea is easy to spot: A thick layer of orange fuzz covers the underside of its leaves. Bog rosemary has silvery blue leaves with snow-white undersides. Leatherleaf, with its dotted yellow elliptical leaves, is one of the most common bog plants; its trailing stems and roots form the supporting network for the floating mat. Don't miss the "peek hole" (stop number eight in the trail guide), from which you can pull a long stick to see just how deep the mat is.

Among the heath plants grows the insect-eating pitcher plant, with its tubular leaves and red flower, big as a silver dollar, bending from a slender stem. Lining the boardwalk is bog laurel – tiny, bell-shaped pink flowers clustered against dark green leaves. And spiky white tufts of bog cotton float on slender green stalks. Stunted tamaracks – one of the few trees that can tolerate this harsh environment – stand scattered across the heath like gnarled black fingers pointing at the sky.

To do: bog walk (trail guide available at trailhead). For information about the bog and other trails in New London, contact the New London Town Hall, Seamans Road, New London, NH 03257; 603-526-4046. Or stop at the information booth on Main Street, opposite the New London Inn.

SAINT-GAUDENS NATIONAL HISTORIC SITE

The home of one of America's greatest sculptors, including its

WHAT IS A BOG?

Most bogs began as shallow ponds, created by the retreating glacier about 10,000 years ago. Amphibious plants, anchored at the shoreline, slowly but steadily spread across the surface of the open water until, eventually, the original pond disappeared. Unlike swamps, which generally have some sort of drainage, bogs tend to be surrounded by higher ground and have poor drainage. The water trapped below the floating mat is so low in oxygen that bacteria responsible for plant and animal decomposition cannot survive. The resulting buildup of undecayed debris, as well as the predominantly acid granitic rock that surrounds most bogs, creates an environment so low in nutrients and so severely acidic that the appearance of a northern bog is distinctive. Only about two dozen species are able to survive in this harsh environment.

The most common bog plant, of course, is the sphagnum moss, or peat moss, which creates the sodlike floating carpet covering the surface of the water. The trailing root systems of leatherleaf and other heath plants anchor in this soggy mass and create the supporting network for the mat. Generally, bog mats are dense enough to support the weight of a human, but horses, cows, and deer have been known to disappear into bogs, never to be seen again. The forest that surrounds the edge of a bog mat, gradually invading it over the years, consists primarily of black spruce and tamarack, hardy conifers adapted to waterlogged, peaty soils.

The two bog plants of greatest interest to most people are the insectivorous species. Pitcher plants catch insects in their red-veined, tubular leaves lined with tiny, downward-pointing hairs. Eventually the insects fall into the small pool of water at the bottom of the leaf, to be digested by enzymes. The minuscule sundew plant entraps insects on sticky hairs that cover its spoon-shaped leaves. As the hairs bend slowly inward, they carry the victim to the surface of the leaf, where digestive enzymes go to work. Although both these plants carry on photosynthesis, the insects provide a supplementary source of nitrogen in the nutrient-deficient habitat of the bog.

surrounding gardens, fields, and woods, is the only National Park Service property in New Hampshire.

Directions: Take I-89 to Exit 20 and drive south on State 12A. The entrance to the Saint-Gaudens site in Cornish is 2.5 miles north of the covered bridge.

It makes sense that sculptor Augustus Saint-Gaudens did most of his best work here in Cornish. Sit for a minute on the wide veranda of the sculptor's home and you'll figure out why. A wide meadow, crisscrossed by birds in flight, stretches away from the house to the edge of a thick woods. Mount Ascutney looms to the west – framed, just so, between classical porch pillars. Grape leaves rustle overhead, a luxuriant ceiling of summer green. In the garden, peonies bow their bright heads, damp and fragrant in the morning sun. It is, above all, quiet.

"People feel at peace here," says John Dryfhout, an authority on Saint-Gaudens who has worked as superintendent of the site for twenty-five years. "They love the fact that it's hidden. It's a discovery. And then it becomes a treasure to those who find it." Saint-Gaudens himself felt he had discovered a treasure when this spot became his summer residence in 1885. He was thirty-seven and had spent years working in a studio in urban settings. "He never picked up his head enough to look around," says Dryfhout, "but he didn't realize this until he came to Cornish. Saint-Gaudens surprised himself by how overwhelmed by nature he was."

When he arrived, the sculptor and his wife, Augusta (they called each other "Gus" and "Gussie"), remodeled the house, converted the barn to a studio, and, over the years, took painstaking care of the grounds. The six-foot pine and hemlock hedges that line the walks and enclose the gardens are evidence of the sculptor's touch. In front of the house stands the State Champion honey locust tree, the largest of its kind in New Hampshire, planted a century ago by the sculptor himself. Though not precisely as Saint-Gaudens knew them, the formal gardens (see box below) between the house and the studio bloom from June through October. And a self-guided interpretive trail leads visitors through the woods and along the brook where the sculptor and his assistants once took breaks from their studio work.

For two decades Saint-Gaudens lived and worked in this rural setting, and other artists followed him to the area. Known as the Cornish Colony, the group included a steady stream of assistants, as well as many of the sculptor's talented friends. When he died in 1907, Saint-Gaudens left behind an impressive

---

THE GARDENS OF AUGUSTUS SAINT-GAUDENS

Peonies, delphiniums, hollyhocks, phlox, fall asters, iris—these are what former Saint-Gaudens gardener Bill Noble calls "the backbone plants" of the gardens, the ones that have been here the longest. "Some of the iris and peonies were probably there when Saint-Gaudens was." While the formal garden has changed through the years, having been redesigned and scaled back, the landscape today reflects the work of two generations either familiar with Saint-Gaudens or dedicated to the spirit of the place.

The spirit of the place, of course, was shaped by the artist, who was a gardener with a vision—a grand vision. His "garden" went well beyond the borders of the flower beds. "Saint-Gaudens saw the whole twenty-five acres as a garden," says Noble. "His was a very active landscape, built to be used." The view of Mount Ascutney, the distant ridges, and the wide-open sweep of lawn, which he used as a golf course—this was all part of it. Accustomed to considering the placement of his large outdoor works, Saint-Gaudens planned his Cornish landscape without the help of landscape architects, giving careful attention to the same features—light and shadow, space and texture—that went into his work as a sculptor. The result was, in fact, a work of art.

---

body of work, some of which is on display here, inside and out. But he also left gardens, fields, woods, and hills for us to contemplate. This landscape itself is a work of art: color and light, shadow and contour and texture, all of it clothed in serenity.

To do: woods trails, garden paths, house tours. Minimal fee. The site is open May 31 through October 31. Call for times. For more information, contact Saint-Gaudens National Historic Site, RR 3, Box 73, Cornish, NH 03745; 603-675-2175.

HELEN WOODRUFF SMITH SANCTUARY

This thirty-acre sanctuary, property of the Meriden Bird Club, is a popular walking spot among local residents and is an easy side trip if you are visiting the Saint-Gaudens site.

Directions: From State 120 in Meriden, go west on Main Street at the blinking yellow light toward Kimball Union Academy. Drive up and over the hill; as you begin to descend, watch for the sanctuary entrance on the right.

The story of the Meriden Bird Club begins in 1910, when naturalist Ernest Harold Baynes delivered a lecture in the Kimball Union Academy chapel. At a time when birds were being killed for collections, for hat plumes, for eggs, and for food, the enthusiasm he generated – and the money that was raised – helped to establish the Meriden Bird Club, devoted to "the protection of our local birds. . . ." The sanctuary – the first of its kind in the nation – was established the following year on an old farm purchased with funds donated by Helen Woodruff Smith. Meriden became known everywhere as the "bird village," and the local activity sparked the formation of hundreds of community bird clubs throughout the country.

On September 12, 1913, the sanctuary was dedicated with a masque (a medieval play) written by poet Percy MacKaye, one of the Cornish Colony artists. Other members of the cast came from the colony and also included the two daughters of President Woodrow Wilson, who came from his nearby summer White House. The site of the masque, which promoted the protection of birds, is marked along the trail with a bronze birdbath made by Annetta Saint-Gaudens (sister-in-law of the famous sculptor).

Today, an early morning walk through the mostly forested sanctuary is accompanied by the sweet, flutelike songs of hermit and wood thrushes. Watch for the flash of an indigo bunting in the small field at the edge of the woods; the bright eyes of a small raccoon, peering from its den in a giant sugar maple; the thread-like delicacy of a maidenhair fern. Several birdhouses and bird-baths along the way are reminders of the local birds that inspired the preservation of this small plot of land – and the far-reaching consciousness-raising that accompanied it.

Trail maps are available at the Meriden Library. For more information, contact the Meriden Bird Club, RR 2, Box 579, Cornish, NH 03745.

MOUNT CARDIGAN

From this open summit, it feels as if a bit of the White Mountains had been plunked down here in west-central New Hampshire.

Directions: From Canaan, drive .5 mile north on State 118 and turn right at the "Cardigan State Park" sign. Bear right at 2.7 miles; bear left at 3.4 miles; at 4.1 miles, you'll come to the park-ing and picnic area and the West Ridge trailhead.

The rounded, naked summit of Mount Cardigan (3,121 feet) rises from the earth like some distant satellite of the White Moun-tains farther north. "Old Baldy" earned its nickname in 1855, when fire stripped the upper slopes and lowered the treeline.

Most of the way, you'll be hiking across 400-million-year-old schist, typical of much of New Hampshire's bedrock. But near the fire tower at the summit, you'll be standing on white slabs of granite called Kinsman quartz monzonite, the same rock that occurs in Lost River Gorge in Kinsman Notch (see page 142).

Much of the mountain lies within 5,000-acre Mount Cardigan State Park. The West Ridge Trail, which leaves from the park picnic area on the west side of the mountain, is the easiest and most direct route to the summit. A multitude of other climbs, of varying difficulties, begin at the Appalachian Mountain Club (AMC) lodge on the east side of the mountain. You may also want to explore the mountain's South Peak (2,900 feet) and Firescrew (3,040 feet), both of which offer splendid views.

Contact the AMC Cardigan Lodge, RFD Bristol, NH 03222; 603-744-8011; or New Hampshire Division of Parks and Recreation, P.O. Box 856, Concord, NH 03302; 603-271-3254.

PARADISE POINT NATURE CENTER
The northern shore of Newfound Lake is bordered by forty-three acres of forests and 3,500 feet of undisturbed shoreline – a good spot for walking beneath giant hemlocks or learning about loons at the interpretive center.

Directions: From Bristol, go north on State 3A nine miles through East Hebron. Turn left on North Shore Road. After a mile, watch for the Nature Center sign and driveway on the left.

At the Paradise Point Nature Center you almost forget you are inside. Everywhere there is news of the natural world: One exhibit explains why loons have red eyes, why loon chicks ride on the backs of their parents, and other loon trivia. An exhibit on wingspans uses pull strings to illustrate the difference between the sizes of bald eagles and hummingbirds – and several species in between. "Keep on Trackin" tests your knowledge of animal tracks. You can learn about the oldest-known eastern box turtle, which lived 138 years, or stand eye-to-eye with an injured barred owl that now lives on the porch here at the edge of the woods. At dusk, he still calls out: "Who cooks for you? Who cooks for you all?" From the woods, its call is returned, again and again, like an endless echo.

A cluster of knobby walking sticks by the door is a reminder that there's more outside. The hand-lettered sign asks simply that you return the stick you use so it's available for the next person. "Most people like the Lakeside Trail," says director Scott Fitzpatrick, "but my personal favorite is the Elwell Trail, which cuts through the heart of the property. I love the old-growth hemlock." Some of these giants, the longest-lived of New Hampshire's native trees, are 300 years old. On a sunny day, hemlock light – clear and green – spills across the needled floor, arches over moss-covered boulders, and slants along tree trunks. At The Point, where the Elwell and Lakeside trails merge, a ledge looks out across Newfound Lake, considered to be among the cleanest lakes in the world. The Lakeside Trail then continues back to the nature center.

To do: bird-watching; nature trails; indoor interpretive center for children and adults; Audubon nature store. The center is open daily from late June through Labor Day and weekends in the spring and fall. Call for hours. For more information and a trail guide, contact the Paradise Point Nature Center, North Shore Road, East Hebron, NH 03232; 603-744-3516; or contact the Audubon Society of New Hampshire, 3 Silk Farm Road, Concord, NH 03301; 603-224-9909.

Hebron Marsh Wildlife Sanctuary. Just down the road from Paradise Point, toward Hebron, is the Hebron Marsh Wildlife Sanctuary. There is no trail, but an observation platform, built into the branches of an old tree, looks out across the wide marshlands on the northwest side of Newfound Lake. Settle in on the platform with binoculars or spotting scope and watch for great blue herons, wood ducks, pied-billed grebes, buffleheads, hooded mergansers, northern harriers, osprey — and more.

White Mountains

The clearest way into the Universe
is through a forest wilderness. Climb the mountains
and get their good tidings. Nature's peace
will flow into you as sunshine flows into trees.
The winds will blow their own freshness into you,
and the storms their energy, while cares
will drop off like autumn leaves.

— John Muir

John Muir knew the power of a mountain. And he knew that the only way to discover this power was to spend time among the peaks, walking through forests, listening to streams, and looking — at rocky ledges, at tiny wildflowers, at unfolding vistas. The White Mountains are ideal for discovering the drama and beauty of a mountain landscape, but if you want to make this discovery alone, or at least in a relatively quiet spot, you have to go your own way.

"Too many people only think of the Presidential Range when they think of the White Mountains," says Buzz Durham, education officer for the White Mountain National Forest. "But there are so many other places, more lightly used, where you don't have to wait in line." Ironically, some of the most crowded parts of the White Mountains are the areas that have been set aside as "wilderness." The dilemmas faced here, the issues of use and overuse, have become acute (see box, page 116).

The following hikes and walks, just a few of hundreds in these mountains, all come recommended by people who know the mountains well, who love them and want others to love them, too. But they are people sharply aware of the dangers of overuse. As you go, be conscious of where you walk — and of how you walk. Be conscious of the land itself. For it is these mountains themselves — these "great cathedrals of the earth," as Ruskin called them — that announce "the good tidings."

Note: Remember that the White Mountains can be as harsh as they are beautiful. Quickly changing weather, higher elevations, and rougher footing make many of the hikes suggested here more difficult than others in this book. See pages xix to xxi for more information before you go.

WHITE MOUNTAINS SOUTH

SANDWICH RANGE WILDERNESS AREA

The village of Wonalancet — what there is of it — sits at a sharp bend in the road near a wide hayfield. At one end of the field, a tiny white chapel is the only spot of color against the deep green hills. Close on all sides, the peaks of the Sandwich Range fill the horizon like huge shadows. Mount Chocorua, Mount Paugus, Mount Passaconaway — the names recall a time when these mountains were known only to the Pequawkets and Penacooks who once inhabited this land.

Another series of peaks known as Sleeper Ridge is named after Katherine Sleeper Walden, a local innkeeper and ardent

SAVING THE FOREST:
A BRIEF HISTORY OF THE WHITE MOUNTAIN NATIONAL FOREST

During the late nineteenth century, the thickly forested peaks of New Hampshire's White Mountains seemed doomed for destruction. Unlike the western forests, which were publicly owned, the eastern forests had been gradually sold off as unwanted land, and by 1867 they were all in private hands. By the 1880s, wood fiber was in demand for paper production, railroads had made the mountains accessible, and the invention of the portable steam sawmill had spurred production. But most of the state's land had long before been cleared for farming; only the mountains remained. By 1890, more than 800 sawmills were churning up the mountain forests.

The loggers who worked the land cut it clean — every tree on a slope, top to bottom. They left behind only slash. Sparks flying from trains and lightning strikes often set fire to the debris, burning thousands upon thousands of acres. The logging exhibit at the Weeks estate (see page 167) in Lancaster describes this period in the history of New Hampshire's forests: "It was a time of large fortunes made and lost, a time of tree slaughter, and a time of fires unequaled before or since. It was also a time of grave concern and eventual opposition by thoughtful individuals to such massive destruction."

When the Society for the Protection of New Hampshire Forests (Forest Society) was founded in 1901, the state owned exactly five acres of public land. One of the earliest environmental organizations in the country, the Forest Society, together with the Appalachian Mountain Club and others, began the battle against public apathy, the large timber operators, and reluctant state and national legislatures. In 1911, after forty-eight attempts, the Weeks Act finally became law. Spearheaded by New Hampshire congressman John Weeks and formally known as the Appalachian–White Mountains Forest Reservation Bill, the law authorized the federal government to purchase lands to be "permanently reserved, held, and administered as national forest lands" for the protection, development, and use of their natural resources.

Interestingly, had it not been for the heavy logging, the forest fires — and the outrage they inspired — the protection of the state's forests would not have come in time to save them. In the decades since the enactment of the Weeks Law, the White Mountain National

Forest—the largest tract of public land in New England—has grown to 769,147 acres. It includes most of the Northeast's highest peaks, more than twenty campgrounds, 1,267 miles of hiking trails, forty-five lakes and ponds, and 750 miles of fishing streams.

This national forest, like all others, is a multiple-use area. Along with absorbing six million visitors a year, it is also a working forest. About 350,000 acres of the land is available for harvesting, although only about 3,000 acres are harvested in any given year. About one-seventh of the forest—the 114,932 acres designated as wilderness—can never be logged (see page 116). Today the Forest Society, along with countless other individuals and groups, continues its fight for the protection of New Hampshire's undeveloped land.

---

conservationist who started the Wonalancet Outdoor Club (WODC). Now a century old, the WODC played an active role in establishing the 26,000-acre Sandwich Range Wilderness. The club publishes a map of the area and maintains forty-nine miles of trails, some of which start at the club's informational kiosk just down the road past the chapel. All of local history seems concentrated right here in this spot—at the base of Mount Wonalancet, named for a Penacook chief; on the edge of the 1984 wilderness area; at the head of a trail system begun in the nineteenth century.

Contact the White Mountain National Forest Saco Ranger Station, RFD 1, Box 94, Conway, NH 03818; 603-447-5448. Consult the map published by the WODC, Wonalancet, NH 03897.

Mount Chocorua
Directions: From State 16, take Fowler's Mill Road, which runs along Chocorua Lake, to Paugus Mill Road. The Liberty Trail begins at the end of the road by the parking area, just before the gate.

In his book *The White Hills*, published in 1859, Thomas

Starr King praised the jagged peak of Mount Chocorua as "everything a mountain should be." Still one of the most popular mountains in New Hampshire, Mount Chocorua (3,475 feet) is not a peak for those seeking to be alone. "If you want to do it," says one local resident, "definitely avoid the Piper Trail. The Champney Falls Trail is busy, too, but pretty with its waterfalls." Many who climb the mountain often recommend the Liberty Trail, built more than a century ago, as a good ascent to the pink-granite summit. The Chocorua Mountain Club (CMC) publishes the sort of detailed summit map you'd like to find for every mountain with a panoramic view: one that identifies all the visible peaks and their elevations.

Contact the CMC, Chocorua, NH 03817. **Note:** *Trails start from several points, intersecting and overlapping on the way; consult the* AMC Guide *before you go. Distance from Paugus Road to summit via Liberty and Brook trails: 3.9 miles; time: three hours forty minutes.*

Big Rock Cave

Directions: The trailhead is just off State 113A in Wonalancet, .3 mile from the bend in the road at the Wonalancet chapel.

This is a hike for cave lovers. The wooded trail begins on an old logging road, gradually narrowing to a footpath that ascends gradually over Mount Mexico's flat summit. The trail connects eventually with the Old Paugus Trail, passing Big Rock Cave on the way. But the jumble of glacial erratics – a boulder cave perfect for exploration – makes a fine destination in itself.

Follow the Cabin Trail for .3 mile to the Big Rock Cave Trail. Distance from here to cave: 1.6 miles; time: seventy minutes.

Mount Israel

Directions: From State 113 in Center Sandwich, follow Sandwich

Notch Road, bearing right after 2.5 miles at the sign for Mead Base (Explorer Scout Camp). Drive another .1 mile to the camp, an old white house, where the Wentworth Trail begins.

Lib Crooker has hiked every 4,000-footer in the White Mountains — and plenty more besides. Mount Israel (2,630 feet), just minutes from her Center Sandwich home, is still one of her favorites. "You just can't get a better view of the Sandwich Range," says Crooker. "It stands alone, so it's often overlooked by hikers who want a ridge experience, but it's a wonderful little mountain."

Note: This mountain could be done as a loop that includes part of the Sandwich Notch Road, climbs the Guinea Pond and Mead trails, and descends along the Wentworth Trail. (See Daniel Doan's Fifty More Hikes in New Hampshire.*)*

Distance from Mead Base to summit: 2.1 miles; time: one hour fifty-five minutes.

Sandwich Notch Road

Directions: This eleven-mile road runs between State 113 in Center Sandwich and State 49 between Campton and Waterville Valley. Not maintained in winter, it is rough, winding, and narrow, but passable — at 15 or 20 mph. And it's a good road for walking.

The road through Sandwich Notch, built in the early 1800s, once was a busy thoroughfare between the northern villages and larger southern cities. But by the time of the Civil War, most of the farms that lined this road were abandoned, and today the notch is deserted, its human history reclaimed by the forest.

Explorers along this road should stop at Cow Cave and Beede Falls, 3.4 miles up the Notch Road from Center Sandwich. Dark and dank beneath an overhanging slab of granite, the cave was made famous by a cow that supposedly wandered from

WHAT IS WILDERNESS?

"A wilderness . . . is hereby recognized as an area where the earth and its community of life are untrammeled by man, where man himself is a visitor who does not remain." So declared the Wilderness Act, passed in 1964 by the United States Congress. The law set aside thousands of acres of federal land for preservation and conservation, including the Great Gulf in the White Mountain National Forest. The Presidential/Dry River was designated as wilderness in 1975, followed by the Pemigewasset and Sandwich Range in 1984. And in 1991, the Caribou–Speckled Mountain area was added to the list.

Unlike most National Forest land, road construction and timber harvesting are not allowed in designated wilderness areas. Mechanized vehicles (including bicycles), power tools, and, with a few exceptions, permanent structures are also prohibited. This is all in keeping with the law, which declared wilderness to be ". . . an area retaining its primeval character and influence, without permanent improvements or human habitation, which is protected and managed to preserve its natural conditions. . . ."

Ironically, designated wilderness areas have become some of the most heavily traveled parts of the mountains. The very effort to preserve these lands can encourage the overuse that harms them, as more and more people set out in search of unspoiled solitude. In some cases, wilderness management may require the closing of trails and other restrictions, in an effort to protect them. "The clash of wilderness preservation versus use and enjoyment by thousands is inherently unresolvable," conclude Guy and Laura Waterman in their book *Wilderness Ethics*. "But that does not absolve any of us from striving to resolve it, from doing the best our generation can to preserve the spirit of wildness" (see page xxiv).

its field late in the year. Before it could be found, winter set in. The cow spent the cold months here, surviving on moisture that dripped from the rock and nibbling nearby vegetation, emerging unscathed the following spring. At the other end of Sandwich Notch, 2.3 miles from the road's intersection with State 49,

Upper Hall Pond is a pleasant picnicking and canoeing spot. (See Steven Smith's *Ponds and Lakes of the White Mountains*.)

WATERVILLE VALLEY AREA

Waterville Valley is no more than five miles, as the crow flies, from Sandwich. But if you follow the main roads around the mountains — southwest on State 113, north on I-93, northeast along State 49 into the valley — you have to travel forty miles. Known mostly for its ski area and its condominiums, the valley also has green spots worth exploring.

Contact the White Mountain National Forest Pemigewasset Ranger Station, RFD 3, Route 175, Plymouth, NH 03264; 603-536-1310. Consult Hiking Trails in Waterville Valley, *published by the Waterville Valley Athletic and Improvement Association. Copies are available from the Waterville town offices or from the Jugtown Country Store in Waterville.*

Welch and Dickey Mountains

Directions: Follow State 49 for 4.5 miles from its junction with State 175. Turn left onto Upper Mad River Road and drive .7 mile. Orris Road forks to the right (at the "Welch Mountain" sign); follow it .6 mile and take the short right fork to the parking area.

The Welch-Dickey Loop Trail in Waterville Valley is popular for a reason: moderate effort, lots of views. The trail crosses both Welch (2,605 feet) and Dickey (2,734 feet) mountains, with ledgy lookouts that keep you in the open for half the trip. "This is my favorite mountain in New Hampshire," says one hiker who's covered more than 900 miles of trails in the White Mountains.

If you can take your eyes off the scenery long enough to notice, you'll find here on the summit one of only four natural communities of jack pine in the state (see box, page 118). There's

evidence here, too, of the glacier: long scrape marks called striations, as well as crag and tail marks, or "chatter marks," where
glacial boulders have rotated and gouged the rock.

*Distance from parking area: 4.4 miles; time: three hours
ten minutes (complete loop).*

East Pond

Directions: From Exit 31 off I-93, drive 5.1 miles east on Tripoli
Road. Turn left to the parking area, 200 feet in.

This moderate woods hike can be combined with Little East
Pond to make a longer trip. Or you can simply head straight for
larger East Pond with its movie-set backdrop — the dark, fir-
covered Scar Ridge. The wagon-road trail that leads to East
Pond winds first through a northern hardwood forest of maple,
beech, and yellow birch. As you walk, watch for the change to
white birch, a sun-loving pioneer species that is one of the first
trees to sprout on open logged-over slopes. The shade-tolerant
balsam fir growing up beneath the canopy eventually will take
over, crowding out the birch and reforesting these slopes with the
conifer forest of prelogging days. East Pond itself has recently
been enlarged by beaver, which returned after a thirty-five-year

---

JACK PINE

The jack pine is a phoenix tree. Like pitch pine, which grows in
sandy soils at lower elevations (see box, page 87), jack pine's serotinous cones usually need fire, at least 160°F, to drop their seeds.
The tree, which is at the southern end of its range here in New
Hampshire, thrives on ledgy outcrops and grows in only four places
in the state: Carter Ledge on Mount Chocorua, Mount Webster in
Crawford Notch, in scattered clumps around Lake Umbagog, and
on the summits of Welch and Dickey, which last burned in 1880.

---

absence. (See Steven Smith's *Ponds and Lakes of the White Mountains.*)

Distance: 1.4 miles; time: sixty-five minutes.

The Scaur

Directions: From I-93, Exit 28, drive ten miles on State 49 to Tripoli Road in Waterville Valley. Turn left, go two miles, and turn right. Cross the bridge and bear left to the parking area. The route to the Scaur begins along the Livermore and Greeley Ponds trails.

The Scaur is more of a rock outlook than a mountain, but the climb up is short and steep, and it's surrounded on all sides by up-close views: Mount Osceola, Mount Tripyramid, and Mount Tecumseh. To do a loop, descend along the Kettles Path, past a series of small kettlehole ponds, and follow the gravel road .6 mile to your car. Watch for the Big Pines Path on your right, partway along the road, and take a short detour in among the towering white pines. (The Kettles Path offers a more gradual ascent to the Scaur.)

Follow the Livermore Trail, a gravel road, .3 mile, turn left on the Greeley Ponds Trail for .7 mile, and then bear right on the Scaur Trail for another .6 mile. Distance to summit: 1.6 miles; time: ninety minutes.

Jennings Peak

Directions: The Sandwich Mountain Trail begins just off State 49, .4 mile southwest of where it meets Tripoli Road.

Sometimes you don't have to go all the way to the top to get a great view. Jennings Peak (3,460 feet) clings to the edge of the Sandwich Range Wilderness about two-thirds of the way up Sandwich Mountain, also known as Sandwich Dome. On the way, you'll climb steadily, but you'll be rewarded with views at

Noon Peak, about halfway along. There are several more look-outs along the ridge as you head toward your destination, which actually offers wider views than the summit itself.

Distance: three miles; time: two hours thirty minutes.

WHITE MOUNTAINS CENTRAL

KANCAMAGUS HIGHWAY AREA

"The problem with the Kancamagus Highway," says Dick Hamilton, president of White Mountains Attractions in Lincoln, "is that most people who drive it, never get off it." This famous 34.5-mile stretch of road (State 112), a National Scenic Byway that winds along the Swift River, is notoriously busy: In summer, mini-parking lots form near popular swimming spots; in fall, carloads of "leaf peepers" creep around each bend. If you'd like to get to know this beautiful road — by "getting off of it" — here's where to go.

Bear Notch Road

Directions: From State 16 in Conway, turn left onto State 112, the Kancamagus Highway. After thirteen miles, turn right onto Bear Notch Road, which meets US 302 after 9.3 miles.

If you are ever trapped on "the Kanc," wishing you had chosen the road less taken, watch for the sign for Bear Notch — and take it. This is your escape. The winding, nine-mile road is paved, but it is rough in spots and not plowed in winter, so it's a much-less-traveled route. The outlooks along the way are beautiful. To the south lies the Sandwich Range. To the north you'll see Mount Willey, Mount Washington, Montalban Ridge, Carter Dome, Wildcat Mountain, and a whole string of other peaks stretched out across the sky.

The road follows the route of the old Bartlett & Albany

logging railroad, which ran here from 1887 to 1894. At the north end of the notch is the Bartlett Experimental Forest, a U.S. Forest Service research site. The road through the forest, past different types of woodlands and wildlife habitats, makes a worthwhile educational detour.

Interpretive guides are available at the White Mountain National Forest Saco Ranger Station at the Conway end of the Kancamagus Highway, RFD 1, Box 94, Conway, NH 03818; 603-447-5448.

Table Mountain

Directions: The Attitash Trail to Table Mountain begins off Bear Notch Road, 2.7 miles south of US 302.

On October 16, 1984, fire broke out on Table Mountain (2,710 feet). For six days the flames roared, burning 106 acres. A decade later, the rebirth of the forest is under way. Birch and aspen, which thrive in open fields, grow thickly through much of the burned-over area, their strong root systems having survived the inferno. But near the trail, which follows the fireline, you'll notice a distinctly different type of forest. When firefighters built the holding line, clearing it of brush and shrubs, they dug down to mineral soil, scraping the area clean of flammable organic material. Today spruce and fir are coming in here, trees that can survive in nutrient-poor mineral soil.

Distance: 1.9 miles; time: 100 minutes.

Hedgehog Mountain and Mount Potash

Directions: The trails to Hedgehog and Potash start at the same point, just off the Kancamagus Highway (State 112), across from the Passaconaway Campground. Park at the kiosk.

The UNH trail up Hedgehog Mountain loops around for a comfortable afternoon hike and includes impressive views from the summit (2,530 feet) southward to the back side of the Sand-wich Range — especially Mount Passaconaway. Allen's Ledge, about a mile up the west (right) side of the loop, offers a resting spot as you climb — or, if you do the loop in reverse, a last-chance look at Mount Chocorua on the way down. (If you are really pressed for time, Allen's Ledge is an easy twenty-five-minute destination in itself.)

Right next door, Mount Potash (2,670 feet) sits just on the edge of the Sandwich Range Wilderness. Its ledges, with wider views than Hedgehog's, are perfect for resting and contemplating the peaceful expanse of green stretching out below, forever pro-tected from chain saws and development.

Round-trip distance along UNH trail to summit of Hedge-hog: about 4.8 miles; time: three hours fifteen minutes. Distance to summit of Potash: about 1.9 miles; time: seventy-five minutes.

East Branch Truck Road
Directions: This gravel road (closed to vehicular traffic) leaves the Lincoln Woods Information Center off the Kancamagus Highway (State 112), 4.1 miles east of I-93, just past the bridge over the East Branch of the Pemigewasset River.

Rocky perches overlooking a river; views to the south of the sharp-edged Scar Ridge; views to the north of Mount Flume, Owl's Head, and the Bond Range — this flat, comfortable trek has all these. What it doesn't have is crowds. "The East Branch Truck Road isn't really a hiking trail," writes hiker and columnist Mike Dickerman, "but it provides trampers headed into the Pemige-wasset Wilderness with a welcome respite from the busy Lincoln Woods Trail." For a short, easy walk, hike .5 mile to a path leading left to rocks at the river's edge and views south to Scar Ridge.

Distance: about three miles.

Boulder Loop Interpretive Trail

Directions: Drive six miles west of the White Mountain National Forest Saco Ranger Station at the east end of the Kancamagus Highway (State 112). Turn right through the covered bridge. The trail starts on the left, a short way from the bridge.

This is glacier territory. Like the rest of New Hampshire, this bit of land on the edge of the Moat Range was sandpapered by a thick, rock-filled sheet of ice as it receded across the landscape. Scrape marks in the granite and scattered giant boulders remain as evidence of this icy event that occurred between 50,000 and 15,000 years ago. Along this trail you'll also find evidence of a nor'easter that tore through, uprooting trees and laying them down in the same direction; parallel "sheet joints" in the granite caused by expansion and contraction; and examples of timber management. And there are views from the ledges across the Passaconaway Valley to Mount Chocorua, Mount Passaconaway, Three Sisters, and surrounding peaks. Pick up the White Mountain National Forest interpretive guide before you set out. *Distance for complete loop: 3.1 miles; time: two hours.*

Greeley Ponds Scenic Area

Directions: From I-93, drive nine miles east on the Kancamagus Highway (State 112). Look for the sign and the parking area on the right. (For a southern approach from Waterville Valley, drive ten miles from I-93, Exit 28, on State 49 to Tripoli Road. Turn left, go two miles, and turn right. Cross the bridge and bear left to the parking area.)

"Greeley Ponds is the closest thing to wilderness you can get in this area," says one local hiker. But it's a popular wilderness — a contradiction in terms that's becoming common, as more and more people go in search of unspoiled landscape (see box, page 116). The best time to try this two-pond hike may be a weekday, or the early morning or the off-season, when you might have the deep green water, the cliffs, and the circling

---

WHAT IS AN OLD-GROWTH FOREST?

"We get complaints all the time about Gibbs Forest," says Dave Govatski of the White Mountain National Forest. "People want to know how come we just leave all those dead trees lying there, but that's one of the characteristics of an old-growth forest." Typically, these stands, usually composed of balsam fir and red spruce, are a mess—a natural mess. They have never been touched by man, but they've been altered by hurricanes and other natural disturbances.

The forest floor is littered with moss-covered blowdowns. Dead trees—standing, leaning, and fallen against one another—create an almost impenetrable maze in the understory. But where enough trees have fallen and an opening has been created in the canopy, sun-loving "pioneer species" such as birch and aspen are growing up. "People usually think 'old growth' means that all the trees are the same age," says Govatski, "but usually you'll see mixed-age trees." What you won't see are stumps left by a chain saw.

One of the best places to see old growth is in the 1,500-acre Gibbs Brook area, along the Crawford Path up Mount Washington. "This is where I send people if they want to see three-toed woodpeckers," says Govatski. "Too many people think a dead tree is a wasted tree. Woodpeckers thrive on these snag trees." The smallest remaining tract of old-growth forest lies close to US 2 on the way in to King Ravine (see page 163). This thirty-six-acre hemlock stand was bought by the Appalachian Mountain Club around the turn of the century to save it from logging. A sample taken recently from a fallen tree indicates that these trees, which thrive in this moist environment, are between 350 and 400 years old.

Other stands of old growth can be found at the Greeley Ponds; on the way to Nancy Pond; in The Bowl Research Natural Area in the Sandwich Range Wilderness; in the Great Gulf Wilderness; and on the back side of Eagle Cliff in Franconia Notch. "Most of these are in spots too difficult to be reached by loggers—and they're few and far between," says Govatski.

stands of old-growth forests all to yourself. The trail between the upper and lower ponds takes you right through old-growth spruce and fir, one of the few places in New Hampshire that the logger's ax never reached. (See box, facing page.)

Distance from the Kanc to ponds: 2.2 miles; time: seventy minutes.

CRAWFORD NOTCH AREA

Crawford Notch bears the name of the most famous family in the history of the White Mountains. In 1819, Ethan Allen Crawford, the legendary "giant of the mountains," worked with his father, Abel, to build the first trail to the summit of Mount Washington. The Crawford Path is still used today. The family also managed several hotels in the area, one of which stood where the Appalachian Mountain Club's Crawford Notch Hostel stands today. *The History of the White Mountains,* written by Ethan's wife, Lucy, tells the story of the family and the mountains.

Today, a six-mile stretch of US 302 cuts through Crawford Notch. En route, it passes the historic Mount Washington Hotel, the Base Road that leads to the Mount Washington Cog Railway, and, on Mount Willey, some of the most famous rock scars in the White Mountains. In 1826, an avalanche sent the Willey family running from their mountainside home in search of safety. The family perished, while their home, secure beneath a rock ledge, survived. The notch itself is formed where Mount Webster (3,910 feet) and Mount Willard (2,850 feet) come together to form a sharp V.

Contact the White Mountain National Forest Ammonoosuc Ranger Station, Trudeau Road (off US 302 north of Franconia Notch), Box 239, Bethlehem, NH 03574; 603-869-2626; or contact Crawford Notch State Park, Willey House Historic Site, Harts Location (off US 302), Crawford Notch, 03575; 603-374-2272.

Elephant Head
Directions: The trail leaves from the east side of US 302, .1 mile south of the Appalachian Mountain Club's Crawford Depot information center.

Before you start this short walk, kids in tow, look up. A giant elephant head peers from the trees, guarding the entrance to Crawford Notch. Its rocky, gray profile is marked with veins of white quartz, creating a trunk, an eye, and other unmistakable elephantine features. The walk to the ledge on top of its head is very short, and the view south into the notch — the same view that was so popular among nineteenth-century painters — is dramatic. Mount Webster and Mount Willard cut a sharp V against the sky. Mount Willard's distinct shape, rounded on one side and sharply angular on the other — the notch side — is a clear example of stoss and lee topography (see box, page 132).
Distance to head from US 302: .2 mile; time: fifteen minutes.

Ammonoosuc Lake
Directions: Park at the Appalachian Mountain Club's Crawford Notch Hostel, just off US 302. The trail begins just off the road that runs behind the building.

At dusk, after rain, on a warm summer night, Ammonoosuc Lake shimmers beneath a fine pink mist. From the far side, as you stand on a steep, pine-needled esker, looking down through drooping hemlock boughs, the peaks of Mount Webster and Mount Willard are perfectly mirrored in the still water. Half-way along the "Around-the-Lake Trail," a side trail leads through the woods, across an old railroad bed, and up a small rise to Red Bench Lookout. Once popular with guests at the Crawford House, one of the notch's grand hotels, this spot has an up-close view of Mount Eisenhower above a break in the trees. You can sit in this historic seat, surrounded by forest, face-to-face with the mountain.

Distance from hostel to bench (or around lake): about one mile; time: forty-five minutes.

Lower Ammonoosuc Falls

Directions: Driving north on US 302, turn right into the unmarked parking area just after Cherry Mountain Road (on right) and just before Zealand Campground.

A short, wide gravel path follows right alongside the Ammonoosuc River and leads to a gushing swirl of water, falling wide and white across the rocks. This is a simple, accessible spot, just off the main road, a gentle place. People walk, fish, take photographs, and sit on strategically placed wooden benches to enjoy the mountain views: the Sugarloafs, Mount Deception, Mount Hale, and Mount Washington. A wheelchair could be pushed along most of the way.

Distance: .5 mile; time: fifteen minutes.

Mount Avalon

Directions: The trail leaves from the Appalachian Mountain Club's Crawford Depot information center, just off US 302.

Mount Avalon stands just behind Mount Willard, one of the most frequently climbed small peaks in the White Mountains. In fact, the trails start at precisely the same place, but most people veer off along the Willard Trail. You can follow the one "less taken" and discover even wider views from the summit of Avalon. The slightly longer trail winds along a brook and includes a short mini-loop to the Pearl and Beecher cascades. Most of the climb is through hardwood forest, but the last .5 mile follows a rocky, conifer-lined stairway to the ledgy outlook at 3,450 feet. Below you'll see Mount Willard; the deep green of Crawford Notch; and in a green valley to the east, the red-roofed Mount Washington Hotel. Mount Tom and Mount Field rise close behind, and the whistle of the Mount Washington Cog Railway drifts across the valley as it puffs its way up the mountain.

Distance to summit: 1.8 miles; time: 100 minutes.

Caps Ridge Trail

Directions: From US 302, take the Cog Railway Base Road and Jefferson Notch Road to the parking area at the top, where the trail begins.

Before you take a single step on this trail, you're already 3,008 feet above sea level – which makes this the highest trailhead on a major highway in the White Mountains. The trail leads to the summit of Mount Jefferson (5,712 feet), and most of it is so strenuous that one hiker has dubbed it "the hike from hell." But there's no reason you can't enjoy the first mile, which is not grueling and which leads to the ultimate picnic spot: a granite outcrop from which you can contemplate the jagged summit of Jefferson and the boulder-strewn Caps Ridge leading up to it. On the first ledge, look for glacial potholes in the bedrock – a sign that the ice sheet buried even these high peaks. The potholes were created by the whirling action of rocks caught in the rush of glacial melt coming off the mountain. To the southeast, on the slopes of Mount Washington, fir waves have left their mark (see box, facing page).

Distance from Jefferson Notch Road to outcrop: one mile; time: fifty minutes.

Zealand Notch

Directions: From US 302, take Zealand Road from the Zealand

THE FIR-WAVE PHENOMENON

According to fir-wave enthusiasts, the northern Appalachians, including the White Mountains, have some of the best fir waves in the world, except maybe for Japan. From a distance, fir waves look like zebra stripes cutting across the slope of a mountain. The silvery gray bands are actually swaths of dead trees, the result of a deadly domino effect thought to be caused by a combination of high wind, shallow soil, and ice accumulation. Fir waves tend to occur at elevations above 2,500 feet, where there is frequent cloud cover.

It begins as a stand of relatively even-aged fir trees. They grow taller and older, competing for nutrients in the thin soil and losing needles as they are battered by the wind. Heavy ice accumulates. Fierce winds blow. The trees weaken until, finally, the first firs topple — onto other weak firs. And down they go, creating a fir wave. These bands of dead trees can be up to thirty feet wide. With the opening of the canopy, new trees begin to grow in the blow-down area, while the mature trees on either side of the fir wave are now exposed to the same winds that toppled their neighbors. And so the fir-wave phenomenon continues, moving five or ten feet a year, uphill or downhill, depending on the prevailing wind.

The best places to see fir waves? "They're commonplace," says the AMC's research director Ken Kimball. "Just scan the upper slopes." Kimball recommends Mount Garfield (4,488 feet), on the edge of the Pemigewasset Wilderness Area, as an ideal climb for a view of the distinct fir waves on North Twin (4,761 feet). The Ammonoosuc Ravine Trail up Mount Washington also provides a good look at fir waves on the slope near the Cog Railway.

Campground. Drive 3.5 miles to the parking area at the end, where the Zealand Trail begins.

Imagine, as you stand amid this green landscape, nothing but grays and blacks — naked soil, charred stumps, exposed rock. No trees. No vegetation anywhere. The fires that raged through Zealand Notch in 1903 consumed more than 10,000 acres. "It still hasn't recovered completely," says Dave Govatski of the White Mountain National Forest. Some of the finest spruce-fir forests in the mountains once grew along these slopes. Stripped first by loggers, then by fire — which raged through the leftover slash — much of Zealand Notch today is thickly forested with paper birch.

But look up at the cliffs of Whitewall Mountain. On the exposed rock face, the fire was so intense that it burned all the soil, and the trees have not returned. The regeneration that occurred through most of the notch will be slower here, and in a few other badly scarred areas, as vegetation struggles to regain a root-hold on the windblown, sun-exposed naked rock.

Distance from Zealand Road to the Zealand Hut: 2.8 miles; time: 100 minutes. Distance from Zealand Hut to Thoreau Falls: about 2.3 miles; time: seventy minutes.

Mount Jackson
Directions: The Webster-Jackson Trail begins on the east side of US 302, .1 mile south of the Crawford Depot information center.

At 4,052 feet, Mount Jackson just squeaked into the 4,000-footer club. Named not for President Andrew Jackson, but for Charles Jackson, a New Hampshire state geologist, this isolated cone is one of the easier big peaks in the White Mountains, and it offers fine views of the southern Presidentials. If you've never climbed a 4,000-footer and are wondering if you are up to it, give this one a try. Be prepared for some rough footing and a final steep scramble to the summit. Bog enthusiasts will want to walk .5 mile north of the summit on the Webster Cliff Trail for a look at Cloudland Bog, which is really two bogs in a minor col at about 3,800 feet. Here you can see alpine bilberry, black crowberry, and the rare cloudberry, which grow at only a few sites above treeline. Be on the lookout for the red-capped spruce

Spruce grouse

grouse among the black spruce and balsam fir. (Stay on the trail in this fragile alpine environment.)

Distance from US 302 to summit: 2.6 miles; time: two hours twenty-five minutes.

Mount Crawford
Directions: From Bartlett, drive about six miles north on US 302.

The Davis Path begins at the paved parking area on the right just beyond the Notchland Inn.

"Crawford is one of the best unknown peaks in the Whites," says Gene Daniell, editor of the *AMC Guide.* "It's not high enough to be on any lists, but the views are outstanding." From the top of Mount Crawford (3,129 feet), you can peer into the notch below, across to the rockslides along Montalban Ridge, and up the Dry River Valley toward the Presidential Range. And Crawford provides a view of the Giant Stairs that climb Stairs Mountain. The series of vertical faults, created two or three hundred million years ago as the mountains formed, were quarried off relatively recently — about 10,000 years ago — as the glacier passed by, neatly removing the weakened rock.

Distance to summit of Mount Crawford: 2.5 miles; time: two hours twenty minutes.

Mount Carrigain

Directions: From US 302, take Sawyer River Road two miles to the Signal Ridge trailhead. Park on the left beyond the Whiteface Brook bridge; the trail begins on the right just before the bridge.

Depending on whom you ask and how you figure it, the summit of Carrigain (4,680 feet) has within its panoramic view precisely the same number of 4,000-foot peaks as — or only one fewer than — Mount Washington itself. Whether or not you can identify all forty-three (or forty-two), the view from this well-situated mountain, well earned after a challenging climb, is

---

SHEEP'S BACKS IN THE MOUNTAINS

Once you begin looking at the White Mountains, you start to notice something. There's a consistency to their topography, an unmistakable repetition of shapes and angles. The northwesterly slopes all tend to be gradual and uniformly flat; the southeasterly slopes are steep and rugged, as if someone had sandpapered the bedrock on one side and hacked away with an ax on the other.

The work, of course, was done by the glacier over thousands and thousands of years. But when the final ice mass retreated, about 10,000 years ago, the shape of the mountains that remained did, indeed, resemble sheep's backs—or, as the French word describes them, *roches moutonnées.* Geologists use the more technical phrase *stoss and lee* to explain this topography. *Stoss* is a Latin derivative meaning "in the face of"; *lee,* as sailors know, describes the side of the boat opposite the wind. Used to describe glacial action, *stoss* refers to the side of the mountain facing the oncoming ice (north or northwest); *lee* refers to the "down-ice" side opposite the flow of the glacier (south or southeast).

"It helps," says Brian Fowler, president of the Mount Washington Observatory and an ice age specialist, "to visualize the glacial ice not as a giant bunch of ice cubes, but as a plastic kind of material that went around and then up and over every surface in its path." On the stoss side, the result was a long, gradual ramp; on the lee side, the oncoming water that just preceded the glacier (unfrozen because of the friction created by the moving ice sheet) spilled down, quickly froze, and, as the ice mass moved on, eventually plucked chunks from the south face of the mountains.

Mount Monroe is a classic example of this topography—"probably the purest you can find in these mountains," says Fowler—best seen from the Bigelow Lawn on Mount Washington or, if you happen to be at a lower elevation, from the base station of the Cog Railway. Mount Adams is also a good example. Smaller examples of "sheep's backs" can be seen on Mount Willard in Crawford Notch, best viewed from the top of Elephant Head (see page 126). The Imp Profile in Pinkham Notch (see page 147) and Cathedral and White Horse ledges in North Conway are also striking illustrations of this geological phenomenon.

Perhaps the most dramatic and easily visible example of glacial carving in the White Mountains is Cannon Mountain, which can be seen from the highway in Franconia Notch. The steep rock cliffs left by the plucking action of the ice have weathered and split over the years, spilling loose chunks of granite down into a huge jumble known as a *talus slope.*

spectacular — especially from Signal Ridge just below the sum-mit, which is wooded. Many feel it's the best in the White Mountains — which, by the way, include forty-eight peaks above 4,000 feet.

Distance from Sawyer River Road to observation platform on summit: five miles; time: four hours fifteen minutes. (This is a full-day hike. Get an early start and go prepared. This trip could also be planned with an overnight stay at Desolation Shelter on the other side of Carrigain, looping back along the Carrigain Notch Trail.)

WHITE MOUNTAINS WEST

FRANCONIA NOTCH AREA

Sandwiched between the Franconia and Kinsman ranges, Fran-conia Notch is the most famous and heavily traveled area in the White Mountains. In 1927, the Society for the Protection of New Hampshire Forests initiated the "Buy a Tree and Help Save the Notch" campaign, which eventually helped spare these 6,000 acres from the logger's ax. The park was dedicated on September 15, 1928, under the watchful eye of the Old Man of the Moun-tains, New Hampshire's most celebrated rock.

Years later, the notch could not be saved from the four-lane highway (I-93) that now provides easy access to many attrac-tions, including the Flume, the Basin, and the craggy Old Man. Probably the busiest trail in this area goes up Bald Mountain and Artist's Bluff, at the northern end of the notch near Echo Lake. This thirty-minute climb, especially popular at sunset, overlooks the wide, U-shaped notch, considered by geologists to be a "textbook glacial trough." The popular Franconia Ridge Trail, although frequently described as "a highway," is beautiful and challenging. (If you do try this one, be prepared; it's not a climb for novice hikers.)

Contact the White Mountain National Forest Ammonoosuc Ranger Station, Trudeau Road (off US 302, north of Franconia Notch), Box 239, Bethlehem, NH 03574; 603-869-2626; or contact Franconia Notch State Park, Franconia NH 03580; 603-823-5563; or the White Mountains Visitors Center, State 112 in Lincoln (P.O. Box 10), North Woodstock, NH 03262; 603-745-8720. For hiking information and a schedule of summer interpretive programs — which include naturalist-led walks — contact Franconia Notch State Park's Hiker Information Center at the Lafayette Campground (US 3, eight miles north of North Woodstock); 603-823-9930.

Mount Pemigewasset

Directions: The Mount Pemigewasset Trail begins at the Flume Visitor Center parking area, just off I-93. The Indian Head Trail begins one mile south of the visitors center, off US 3 south of the Indian Head Resort.

Most people who climb Mount Pemigewasset take the Mount Pemigewasset Trail, which leaves from the Flume Visitor Center parking area. The Indian Head Trail is a less-used alternative that takes only a few minutes longer. The 2,557-foot summit offers great views — down into Franconia Notch and south toward Moosilauke and the Sandwich Dome. Like the famous Old Man of the Mountain, the Indian Head was formed by glacial quarrying.

Distance to summit along Mount Pemigewasset Trail: 1.8 miles; time: ninety minutes. Distance to summit along Indian Head Trail: 1.9 miles; time: 100 minutes.

Georgiana Falls

Directions: From I-93, take Exit 1 for the Flume. Follow US 3 south 2.5 miles to Hanson Farm Road. Drive .1 mile to the parking area. Follow the short dirt road that runs beneath I-93 and then bear right to reach the trailhead, which turns left into the woods.

You hear the water before you see it, but soon the trail is following close to the Harvard Brook. The woods are damp and dark; the hobblebush and striped maple that survive in the understory grow their leaves broad and wide to catch as much sunlight as possible. The trail climbs steadily upward to Georgiana Falls, and then higher still to Harvard Falls — both dramatic cascades in spring. In drier weather, the falls are less gushing, but the gigantic granite boulder formations beneath them are just as impressive.

Distance from Hanson Farm Road: 1.2 miles; time: one hour.

Basin-Cascade Trail and Lonesome Lake

Directions: There are several ascents to popular Lonesome Lake, located in the center of Franconia Notch. The Basin-Cascade Trail, a worthwhile trip in itself, begins at the Basin, just off the Franconia Notch Parkway, slightly south of the Hiker Information Center.

Lonesome Lake probably is one of the best-loved sites in Franconia Notch — and with good reason. In his book *Ponds and Lakes of the White Mountains,* veteran hiker Steven Smith points out that one of the lake's many charms is the view that comes with it: "On a day of sun and shadow the vista across the water to the barren ramparts of Franconia Ridge is so beautiful it's almost surreal. Every detail of ridge and ravine is revealed."

To avoid the busy Lonesome Lake Trail, which starts at Lafayette Campground, try the Basin-Cascade Trail (rough in spots), with short side paths to watery views, including Kinsman and Rocky Glen falls. This is a V-shaped streambed, relatively young compared with the U-shaped glacial notches. When the trail meets the Cascade Brook Trail, you can turn back or continue to Lonesome Lake.

At the lake, you'll be standing on the floor of a shallow glacier-carved basin. Runoffs from the surrounding slopes — and industrious beaver — have maintained this lake for thousands of years, since the ice retreated. Be sure to follow the Around-Lonesome-Lake Trail (.8 mile, twenty-five minutes), which many hikers ignore. Watch for those surreal views. *(Note: If you prefer quiet to crowds, don't plan to make this trip on a lovely summer weekend.)*

Distance from Basin to end of Basin-Cascade Trail: one mile; time: forty-five minutes. Distance from Basin to Lonesome Lake: 2.6 miles; time: one hour fifty minutes.

The Franconia Bike Path and the Rim Trail

Now comes a high-road/low-road choice. The low road, the nine-mile Franconia Bike Path, is paved — easy for walkers and, in some places, for wheelchair users. The path runs the length of Franconia Notch from Lincoln to the Skookumchuck Trail and is used mostly by bikers, but others are welcome. There are several access points along the way, as well as a campground in the middle. (Be alert for bicycle traffic, which can be heavy. In winter, cross-country skiers and snowmobilers use the Franconia Bike Path.)

If you prefer the high road, head for the Cannon Mountain Ski Area, which offers a nonstrenuous way to enjoy the notch: Ride the gondola to the top of Cannon Mountain (4,200 feet) and walk the short Rim Trail at the top, which leads past great outlook ledges to a fire-tower lookout. From this northern point, you can look south into the notch and along the whole Cannon-Kinsman Range.

MOOSILAUKE and KINSMAN NOTCH AREA

This corner of the mountains, west of Franconia Notch, is much quieter than the more popular notches — but equally beautiful. M.F. Sweetser's *White Mountains: A Handbook for Travelers,* first published in 1876 and updated in 1894, includes the Rev. Washington Gladden's description of the Moosilauke area: "I have seen most of the New England scenery, and I give my hearty preference to Moosilauke over every mountain whose top I have climbed. The view from Washington is vast but vague; the view from Lafayette is noble, but it shows us little of the sweet restfulness of the Connecticut valley; on Moosilauke we get all forms of grandeur and all types of beauty." The trips suggested here all lie in the shadow of this great peak.

Mount Moosilauke

Directions: From Tunnel Brook Road (see entry, page 139), drive straight past a hairpin turn at 1.4 miles and continue to the start of the Benton Trail at three miles. The Gorge Brook Trail begins at Dartmouth's Ravine Lodge, at the end of a 1.5-mile access road that begins off State 118 (5.8 miles east of its junction with State 25 in Warren, 7.2 miles west of its junction with State 112 in North Woodstock).

Mount Moosilauke (4,802 feet), the highest peak in this region and the most westerly 4,000-footer in the White Mountains, is indeed, as its Native American name indicates, "a bald place." The rough summit is softened only by a covering of hardy alpine flowers — mountain sandwort, mountain cranberry, and three-leaved cinquefoil. It's hard to imagine, standing alone here, that this peak was once a popular destination for visitors, who arrived in horse-drawn carriages to stay at the Prospect House, built in 1860. They came, clearly, for the view: "the sweet restfulness of the Connecticut Valley," together with the grandeur of the mountain panorama.

There are several choices for an ascent. The Benton Trail — the least-used "backdoor approach" — climbs through all the land zones found in the White Mountains: northern hardwoods, a transition forest, spruce-fir, and alpine tundra.

A loop route to the summit begins along the Gorge Brook Trail, which has fine outlooks, and descends along the Moosilauke Carriage Road and the Snapper Trail. Be sure to check out the views from the less-frequented South Peak, reached via a short side trail at the junction of the Carriage Road and Glencliff Trail. (See Daniel Doan's *Fifty Hikes in the White Mountains.*) Cirque-lovers take note: Joblidunk Ravine, a lower-elevation cirque than those in the Presidential Range, is an example of an "incipient" cirque – less well defined yet noticeably bowl-shaped.

Distance for entire loop: 7.1 miles; time: six hours.

Black Mountain

Directions: The easier Black Mountain Trail begins on Howe Hill Road, off State 116 in Benton. Another more difficult – and scenic – route to the summit, the Chippewa Trail, begins on Lime Kiln Road in North Haverhill. From State 25 in East Haverhill, follow Lime Kiln Road for 3.1 miles, bearing left at a major fork; watch for the trailhead on the right.

One hiker classifies Black Mountain (2,830 feet) – along with nearby Blueberry Mountain (2,662 feet) – as "a great little peak nobody ever seems to climb." True, it's a bit out of the way, but the view from the top – a close-up look at Mount Moosilauke, a panorama of the Connecticut River Valley, and Vermont's rounded Green Mountains – is wonderful. So is the solitude. (See Daniel Doan's *Fifty More Hikes in New Hampshire.*)

Distance up Black Mountain Trail to summit: 1.7 miles; time: ninety minutes. Distance up Chippewa Trail to summit: 1.8 miles; 100 minutes.

Tunnel Brook

Directions: From State 112, drive .5 mile east beyond its junction with State 116 and turn onto Tunnel Brook Road. Continue on this road 3.8 miles to the end of its maintained section, where the trail begins. *Note: The trail is also accessible at its southern end, off State 25.* (See Daniel Doan's *Fifty More Hikes in New Hampshire.*)

This level woods walk comes highly recommended by Mike Dickerman, a 4,000-footer peak-bagging enthusiast who, nevertheless, loves the solitude of what he calls a "lovely valley walk into the slide-scarred notch between Mount Moosilauke and Mount Clough." This westernmost, little-known mountain notch provides dramatic close-up views of steep rock slides, the result of a 1927 avalanche caused by extreme flooding. Count the string of beaver ponds as you go; if you make it to Mud Pond at the very end, you should have passed eight. (See Steven Smith's *Ponds and Lakes of the White Mountains.*)

Distance from Tunnel Brook Road to Mud Pond: 2.1 miles; time: one hour.

Wachipauka Pond

Directions: From State 25 in Warren, drive north to Glencliff and continue .5 mile. Look for the brown hiker sign on the left and park in the pulloff area.

At some point in the nineteenth century, Wachipauka, the Native Americans' "mountain pond," lost its rhythmic moniker and became "Meader Pond." Nevertheless, it *is* a mountain pond – one you can hike to and also look down on. Webster Slide Mountain looms near the edge of the water, and a steep, rough climb (.7 mile) brings you to one of those perfect places: a view outward to mountain peaks, a view downward to the pond. "From this airy perch," writes Steven Smith in *Ponds and Lakes of the White Mountains,* "you look straight down on the pond, which takes the shape of a giant stingray floating in a deciduous ocean." *Distance to pond: 2.3 miles; time: ninety minutes.*

Beaver Brook Cascades
Directions: The Beaver Brook Trail starts off State 112, just beyond the entrance to Lost River. Look for a dirt parking area on the left, almost directly opposite the Kinsman Ridge trailhead across the road.

They keep coming, one after another – each cascade a long, watery veil plunging clear and cold from dark rock ledges. Just when you think you must have reached the very last fall, you haul yourself up yet another steep stretch and gasp in awe – and for breath – at yet another pounding explosion of water in the middle of this deep green woods. If you love waterfalls, you won't want to miss this, but be prepared: The mile-long stretch of trail that leads eventually to the top of Mount Moosilauke is so steep that wooden steps and iron handrails have been drilled into the rock. Experienced hiker and outdoor columnist Mike Dickerman describes this trail as "an unending one-mile-long steep stretch. . . . Beaver Brook to this day ranks as one of my most tiresome mountain ventures." But, oh, those waterfalls. (See Bruce and Doreen Bolnick's *Waterfalls of the White Mountains.*) *Distance to top of falls: 1.1 miles.*

Road through Kinsman Notch
Directions: From I-93 in North Woodstock, drive west on State 112.

The road through Kinsman Notch (State 112) twists through the glacier-carved pass between Mount Moosilauke and Kinsman Ridge – wild and empty compared to nearby Franconia Notch. Two hikes described above, Tunnel Brook and Beaver Brook Cascades, begin along this stretch of road; Beaver Pond, one of the most picture-perfect roadside lakes you'll ever come across, offers a lovely waterside walk. (See Steven Smith's *Ponds and Lakes of the White Mountains.*) Although many people find their way along this road to Lost River Reservation, few continue through the winding pass, making it an uncrowded route – a satisfying autumn alternative to the busy Kancamagus Highway farther east.

Lost River Reservation
Children and adventurous adults can clamber through boulder caves in this steep gorge, the first property purchased by the Society for the Protection of New Hampshire Forests, in 1912. Other features include a nature garden and an ecology path.

Directions: From I-93 or US 3, follow State 112 west toward North Woodstock. Lost River is six miles beyond the town, on the right.

People have been exploring the Lost River Gorge ever since 1852, when young Lyman Jackman disappeared beneath a boulder while fishing. He fell fifteen feet and found himself standing waist-high in water. His brother Royal Jackman hauled him out, unharmed, and, years later, led the first "guided tour" of the gorge. Today's visitors descend into this gorge along carefully constructed wooden stairways and boardwalks – past heaps of giant rocks, plunging waterfalls, and tilted trees gripping boulders in curled, rooty fists – 300 feet down into a misty gray and green world.

Fenris the Wolf, his image cast in stone, stands as guardian of the gorge. At the Hall of Ships, the keel of a sailboat hangs from one rocky wall of the cave, and approaching from the other end is the bow of a huge destroyer – all sculpted in stone. Crawl through the Cave of Odin, dark and damp. Or stand in the Cave of Silence, in the pitch black, and listen to the hush: The river rushes along a few feet beneath the cave, but you can hear nothing. Only the adventurous – and the small – should try the Dungeon or the Lemon Squeezer, caves that require belly squirming

WHAT IS A GORGE?

"Sometimes people don't realize that we didn't create this," says Forest Society naturalist Will McNeill, explaining that the Lost River Gorge was the work of the glacier and of other natural forces. However, this is not a typical U-shaped glacial valley, nor is it a V-shaped ravine slowly carved by a stream. This gorge was created by powerful torrents of glacial meltwater.

About 10,000 years ago, when the glacier began receding, creeping south to north along the top of Kinsman Ridge, drainage westward into the Connecticut River was completely blocked. Instead, the glacial meltwater came tearing through the Lost River Valley, creating a gorge at least fifty feet deep. The debris-laden river scoured and polished the sides of the gorge, creating huge, rounded potholes. When the ice was gone, the river returned to normal depths. But over time, as the rock walls repeatedly froze and thawed, huge chunks of rock broke off along the joint lines and toppled into the gorge, creating caves and ledges.

Most of the gorge is composed of Kinsman quartz monzonite, a grayish granite. But in some places, noticeably lighter bands of rock, called pegmatite dikes, run through the darker rock. These bands penetrated a crack in the granite while it was still molten, cooled quickly, and created large mineral crystals: pieces of red garnet, mica, and rose quartz. More resistant to erosion, pegmatite dikes have created the towering walls at Lost River's Lookoff Point and spectacular Paradise Falls.

and inhaling through the tight spots. From the Bridge of Sighs, lean over and watch the waterfalls plunging down, down, down into the gorge below.

At the top of the gorge is a nature garden, often overlooked by eager cave-seekers. Here in one small space is one of New England's finest collections of native plants, carefully labeled and grouped in several natural communities: a small bog area, an alpine garden, a field, a forest, and a swale (a wet meadow). You'll learn the difference between the cinnamon fern, with its

separate stalk of waving spores, and the nearly identical interrupted fern, with spores that "interrupt" its fronds halfway down
the stem. See the infamous insect-eating pitcher plant and the
beautiful rose azalea. If you time it right (early July), you might
catch the pink-and-white blossoms of the rare showy lady's
slipper. The cluster here is the second-largest in the state.

To do: *gorge viewing, picnicking, nature trail, ecology
trail; gift shop; cafeteria. Owned by the Forest Society and run
by White Mountains Attractions, Lost River is open mid-May
through mid-October. Call for hours and prices. For more information, contact Lost River, Kinsman Notch, North Woodstock,
NH 03262; 603-745-8031.*

WHITE MOUNTAINS EAST

PINKHAM NOTCH AREA

It is here, in Pinkham Notch, that the presence of the most
famous mountain in the East is most strongly felt. Mount Washington seems almost too close here — impossible to fathom. The
6,288-foot peak looms larger-than-life, its top often shrouded in
clouds. Called *Agiochook,* "the dwelling place of the Great
Spirit," by the Abenaki, the mountain was once considered too
sacred to ascend. Not anymore.

Today, an auto road and a steam-powered, mountain-
climbing cog railway twist to the summit from opposite sides of
the mountain. Each year, thousands of people visit the fifty-four-
acre state park at the summit, hoping for a glimpse of what P. T.
Barnum called "the second greatest show on earth." On clear
days — about sixty days a year — the view stretches across four
states and into Canada. It was here at the famous Mount
Washington Observatory, on April 12, 1934, that a 231-mph gust
of wind blew through — the highest wind ever recorded on land.

Most visitors to Pinkham Notch come to climb, drive, or

Rare pink-and-white showy lady's slipper

ride to the top of "the mountain with the snowy forehead"; many are lured by the 4,000-foot summits of the Presidential Range. Impossible as it seems to contemplate now, in 1934 a proposal was made to build a twenty-five-mile "scenic, skyline highway" — from Mount Clinton in Crawford Notch across the summits of Pleasant, Franklin, Monroe, Washington, Clay, Jefferson, Adams, and Madison. Today, although those summits are safe from car traffic, heavy foot traffic through the Presidential–Dry River and Great Gulf wilderness areas is raising serious concerns about how best to maintain the areas John Muir called "the hope of the world."

Contact the White Mountain National Forest Androscoggin Ranger Station, 80 Glen Road, Gorham, NH 03581; 603-466-2713; or contact the Appalachian Mountain Club's Pinkham Notch Camp, P.O. Box 298, Gorham, NH 03581; 603-466-2727.

Square Ledge

Directions: The trail begins opposite the Pinkham Notch Visitors Center. Follow the Lost Pond Trail for 200 feet and then veer left for Square Ledge.

Square Ledge provides what most kids would call an "in-your-face" view of Mount Washington. And this is, as a matter of fact, a good first climb for children, with a steep, narrow scramble through some tight rocky spots and then a reward: views into Pinkham Notch and across to the famed giant of the Presidential Range and the two glacial cirques scooped out beneath the mountain's cone — Huntington and Tuckerman ravines. (For a longer trip, continue along the Lost Pond Trail, which follows the Ellis River and then climbs a bit to reach the pond. More good views here, before you descend and follow the road back to your car.)

Distance to Square Ledge: .5 mile; time: thirty minutes. Add another thirty minutes to get to Lost Pond.

Glen Boulder

Directions: The trailhead is at the Glen Ellis Falls parking area, off State 16, just a few miles south of the Appalachian Mountain Club's Pinkham Notch Hut.

This trail leads, as its name suggests, to a boulder, a gigantic glacial erratic perched on the edge of a ridge, angled so sharply away at its base that it seems the slightest push would send it toppling into the notch below. Geologists have matched the rock type in this boulder with the rock found in Boott Spur, the southwest shoulder of Mount Washington, about a mile north and 600 to 700 feet higher.

The climb to reach the boulder – the shortest route to a point above treeline in Pinkham Notch (see box, page 148) – includes some rough scrambles along a rocky trail that will get you breathing hard. The last few yards are the most satisfying: Out you come from twisted spruce woods, grasping rock with both hands and hauling, breathing hard, eyes on the yellow trail markers ahead, up and around one more rocky corner, and then there it is above you – a precarious sculpture left by the glacier, the entire sky spread out behind it in a wide and shifting backdrop.

Distance to boulder from parking area: 1.6 miles; time: 100 minutes.

Imp Profile

Directions: The northern end of the Imp Trail leaves from State 16, about 2.6 miles north of the entrance to the Mount Washington Auto Road.

The jumbled cliff that forms the Imp Profile (3,165 feet) is best seen from below, near the Dolly Copp Campground at the end of the Pinkham B (Dolly Copp) Road. But climbing the Imp itself provides a great view of Pinkham Notch and the northern Presidentials, along one of the few big loop trails in the notch.

LIFE AT THE TOP

The world above treeline is harsh. Fierce winds, subzero temperatures, blazing sun — this is a land of extremes. Only the tough — and the tiny — survive. The *krummholz* (German for "twisted wood") that creeps across exposed boulders consists of scraggly miniature versions of the tall balsam fir and black spruce found in the forest. The alpine flowers that grow higher still, at 4,500 to 5,000 feet, have developed special survival tactics: They grow close to the ground to avoid the wind and to soak up heat from the soil; many have waxy leaves that retain moisture; some reproduce by sending up shoots from underground instead of by dispersing fragile seed.

Some of the most common alpine flowers include the white, five-petaled diapensia; Labrador tea, whose leaves have rusty, fuzz-coated undersides; and the yellow-flowered mountain avens. The avens, which grows profusely here, is found in only one other place, a small island in Nova Scotia. The most famous alpine flower is the Robbins' cinquefoil (*Potentilla robbinsiana*), one of the rarest species in the United States. It grows in a barren quarter acre on Mount Washington and in a small patch on Franconia Ridge — and nowhere else in the world. When it was discovered here by James Robbins in the early 1800s, the flower grew in four other locations where it is now extinct. In 1980, the Dry River Trail was rerouted in an effort to protect this fragile community.

"If you can time it right," says botanist Frederic Steele, "you'll get a real show. Aim for early to mid-June." Climb to Glen Boulder to see several heath plants: mountain cranberry, Labrador tea, alpine bilberry, and black crowberry. On Mount Washington, in the Alpine Gardens and Cow Pasture (accessible via the Mount Washington Auto Road as well as by trail), diapensia, Lapland rosebay, and alpine azalea bloom in a tufted mass of white and pink.

(When you visit this tundra habitat, stay on the path. Hiking boots are death to alpine plants, some of which require a decade of growth before they can reproduce.)

As you go, you will be treading where glacial ice once did its work: the north (or stoss) side of the mountain (the left side as you look from the Pinkham B Road) slopes gradually to the summit; the Imp peers out from the south (or lee) side of the peak, its defining features plucked out by the glacier as it moved southward (see box, page 132).

Distance around loop: 6.3 miles; time: four hours fifteen minutes. (The ends of the loop are about .3 mile apart, so you'll need to walk a short distance on the highway to get back to your car.)

Carter Notch
Directions: The easiest way in to Carter Notch is along the Nineteen-Mile Brook Trail, which leaves from State 16, about one mile north of the entrance to the Mount Washington Auto Road.

Two tiny lakes, clear and cold; a small stone hut; mountains that drop down steep and green on all sides — Carter Notch (3,388 feet) offers some of the most dramatic scenery in the White Mountains. Lib Crooker remembers hiking this trail in 1922 with her father, Red MacGregor, the first hut manager here for the Appalachian Mountain Club. "This is the very first hike I ever took with him. It's a good day trip, and not really on the way to anywhere, so it doesn't get much use. And you should see it at night, with the stars out, the sky reflected in the two ponds." You should also see it from Pulpit Rock. It's a steep climb, but once you are there, suspended in air above those two lakes, hemmed in on all sides by steep mountain walls, it's hard not to feel reverent.

Distance to the stone hut: 3.8 miles; time: two hours fifty-five minutes.

NORTH CONWAY AREA
North Conway is more famous as home to dozens of name-brand

outlet stores than as a place to wander through the woods identifying endangered plants. Or a place to sit quietly alone at the top of a mountain. Or a place to canoe across a woods-circled pond. The trails described below will get you started on your exploration of "the land beyond the strip." Other spots worth discovering include Mount Doublehead, with its north (3,053 feet) and south (2,939 feet) summits; little Mount Stanton (1,748 feet), with its surprising vistas from Whites Ledge; and North Moat (3,201 feet), a loop hike with good views of the Presidentials.

Contact the White Mountain National Forest Saco Ranger Station, RFD 1, Box 94, Conway, NH 03818; 603-447-5448.

Mount Kearsarge North

Directions: From the rest area at Intervale on State 16, take Hurricane Road 1.5 miles to the start of the shorter Mount Kearsarge North Trail. The longer Weeks Brook Trail starts in South Chatham. From State 113, take South Chatham Road 5.2 miles to the trailhead.

There are two routes to the top of Mount Kearsarge North (3,268 feet): a short one and a long one. The short one, not surprisingly, is the most frequently traveled. The longer one runs past Shingle Pond at about the halfway point. No matter which route you choose, the view from this well-situated mountain, topped by a fire tower, is the same: north to the Mahoosuc Range, west to the Presidentials and the Pemigewasset Wilderness, south to the Sandwich Range. "One of the best views in the mountains," says Buzz Durham of the White Mountain National Forest.

Distance to summit along Mount Kearsarge North Trail: 3.1 miles; time: two hours fifty minutes. Distance to summit along Weeks Brook Trail, past Shingle Pond: 4.9 miles; time: three hours fifty minutes.

Mountain Pond

Directions: From State 16A in Intervale, turn onto Slippery
Brook Road (Town Hall Road) and drive 6.3 miles to the Mountain Pond Loop Trail.

Visit Mountain Pond first in early summer, when it's ringed
in green. Watch for kingfishers, mergansers, and the resident
pair of nesting loons. Listen for cedar waxwings in the woods.
Look for the work of the pileated woodpecker. Notice, as you
walk the loop, how the forest changes – from a cool, damp
coniferous forest on the south side to a drier pine forest on the
more exposed north side. In the middle of it all, the pond lies
shiny and still beneath the summer sun.

And then there's fall. From a mountaintop, color spreads
away into the distance; at Mountain Pond, the color is vivid and
close: yellow birches, red sugar maples, a touch of deep spruce
green. The pond's mirror image doubles the intensity. Walk the
easy Loop Trail. Or, if you want to be in the middle of it all, put
in a canoe. When you reach the center, pull in your paddles, let
the surface settle, and sit surrounded, literally, by water color.

*Distance of loop: 2.7 miles; time: one hour twenty-five
minutes.*

Black Cap

Directions: From State 16, drive 3.7 miles up Hurricane Mountain Road. The Black Cap Path starts just past the altitude sign.

The steep, winding drive up Hurricane Mountain Road to
the Black Cap Path trailhead is remarkable in itself – and does a
lot of the climbing work for you, leading to a starting point that's
2,101 feet high before you've even begun. The short hike from
here to the summit (2,369 feet) winds its way through spruce and
beech forests to "absolutely the best views of the Green Hills –

the easiest climb for the best perspective in the area," according to one fan of this small mountain.

Distance: 1.3 miles; time: fifty-five minutes.

Peaked Mountain (Green Hills Preserve)

The short, moderately steep climb up Peaked Mountain offers views of the White Mountains – and a look at two small endangered plant species.

Directions: From State 16 in North Conway, take Artist Falls Road .5 mile. Turn right onto Thompson Road and continue to the parking area at the end. The Peaked Mountain Path begins across the brook, along the flagged path. Watch for the six-foot boulder where a sharp right turn follows a loop trail, which makes a more interesting ledgy climb to the summit.

Right behind North Conway's strip of outlet stores, fast-food eateries, and steady traffic, Peaked Mountain (1,734 feet), in the midst of The Nature Conservancy's Green Hills Preserve, rises above the crowds and congestion, offering silence and solitude. The trail starts at Artist Falls Brook, once a favorite site among painters of the White Mountain School of Art, who sat in these woods trying to capture the light and movement of mountain-clear water rushing across dark rocks. The path winds through hardwood forest of northern red oak and beech. In the spring, Canada mayflower covers most of the ground, punctuated by dark-leafed wintergreen with its tiny red berries. At one bend in the trail, nestled next to a small boulder, a tiny pink-and-yellow wild columbine dangles from its slender stem.

In less than a mile, the hardwoods give way, and suddenly your boots scrape against open rock. Gnarled pines – red, white, and pitch – stand like stubborn sentinels over giant slabs of granite scoured bare by the glacier. Bent and twisted by the elements, these trees – which thrive in dry, acid soil – seem small

for their age. But they are tough. Some bear the scars of fire —
there have been at least three up here. Many grow to be 125 years
old. One striking specimen is 176.

In the crevices at your feet grow two less spectacular but
more significant plants: mountain sandwort, an alpine flower that
blooms three or four times a year; and silverling, a delicate tan-
gled plant that grows in hand-size clumps and clings to a bit of
soil by a single root (see box below). It would be easy to miss
these unremarkable plants, but they are the reason the preserve

---

SILVERLING
(*Paronychia agricoma* var. *albimontana*)

You might easily mistake it for a weed. But *Paronychia*, commonly
known as silverling, is rare enough to have earned an S3 rating on
the New Hampshire Natural Heritage Inventory (NHNHI) program's one-to-five endangered-species scale (see box, page 56). The
plant doesn't look like much; if you found it growing in your lawn,
you'd probably toss it in the compost without much thought. But it
doesn't grow in lawns. In fact, it grows hardly anywhere. Because
silverling does not compete well with other plants, it occurs mostly
in glacial cracks and rock lines, areas with so little soil that other
species have trouble surviving.

Since it can't compete, silverling must endure scorching sun all
summer, on ledges with little water. In winter, it lives through wind
and subzero temperatures, usually without snow cover. "What fas-
cinates me about it," says preserve manager Peter Benson, "is its
durability under incredibly harsh conditions. Considering where it
grows, its survival is amazing." The Nature Conservancy has located
the lacy green plant, with its nearly indistinguishable green flower,
in only thirteen sites in the White Mountains and one in Massachusetts. One of the best ways to see it is to climb Peaked Mountain
and crouch alongside a crevice in the granite. (Watch where you
walk — silverling's single-roothold makes it very vulnerable to foot
traffic.)

---

is here: Both plants appear on The Nature Conservancy's endangered-species list.

Directly to the north, White Horse and Cathedral ledges, favorite rock-climbing spots, cut jagged scars across the green. The view spreads out across the horizon — Mount Washington, Mount Adams, Mount Carrigain — peak after peak. From this perspective, the town of North Conway looks insignificant. Knowing how close, and how sprawling, it really is makes the preserve seem even more valuable. Overhead, a northern harrier rides the thermals, and except for the wind bending the pines, there is only silence.

Distance to summit (by either side of loop): 1.3 miles; time: seventy-five minutes. For more information and a trail map, contact The Nature Conservancy, Box 119, Glen, NH 03838; 603-383-9153.

EVANS NOTCH AREA

The long road through Evans Notch is narrow and wooded. It twists past mountains that hug close to the road, mountains whose summits — more rounded than the sharp peaks of the Presidentials — seem magnified because of their nearness. Squeezed tightly between the Carter Range and the eastern border of New Hampshire, most of Evans Notch actually lies in Maine and includes the newest wilderness area in the White Mountain National Forest, designated in 1991. But while the two peaks for which the wilderness is named, Caribou (2,828 feet) and Speckled (2,906 feet), lie across the border, the New Hampshire side, less accessible than any other notch in the White Mountains, is a good place for those seeking solitude.

For more information, contact the White Mountain National Forest Evans Notch Ranger Station, RR 2, Box 2270, Bethel, ME 04217; 207-824-2134.

Deer Hill Bog Wildlife Viewing Blind

Directions: From Stowe, drive north 5.2 miles on State 113 and turn right onto Deer Hill Road. (Watch for the "Windagan B&B" sign at the start of this gravel road.) The viewing blind is 2.8 miles down on the right.

Here's where you can practice your patience. If you wait and watch quietly enough, hidden inside the blind, you might see black ducks, wood ducks, mergansers, beaver, moose, or deer. Or perhaps you'll spot a great blue heron, attracted here by the elevated platforms built to encourage the giant birds. These twenty-five acres of wetlands, a skeleton-forest of dead stumps and leaning trunks, are the result of damming – by beaver and humans. Birds are sensitive to color, but inside the blind, you can observe this watery world without being visible. The blind, which sits right at the edge of Deer Hill Bog, has slits in the sides at various heights and is wheelchair-accessible.

Little Deer Hill and Big Deer Hill – Plus a Few More Hills

Directions: Trailheads are located off Deer Hill Road (see above entry) and behind the Appalachian Mountain Club's Cold River Camp, which is on State 113, one mile north of Deer Hill Road.

Little Deer and Big Deer are miniature versions of the giants across Evans Notch. But the ledges on Big Deer (1,367 feet) and even the summit of Little Deer (1,090 feet), only 600 feet above the valley floor, offer dramatic views of the Baldfaces and other high peaks. On the way up, the trail passes two abandoned mines where amethyst and mica were quarried. You can walk the trail in a loop that starts at the AMC Cold River Camp and heads back along Deer Hill Road.

Just south of the two Deer Hills, the Conant Trail, also known as the Pine-Lord-Harndon Trail, takes you in a loop across the three hills that give this trail its name. Along the way, you can explore another mica mine and look down into Horse-shoe Pond. If you listen, you may hear the loons.

Distances: Hikes on these little hills can take as little as thirty minutes or as long as all day. Plan your route and head out.

The Basin
Directions: From State 113 in Hastings, follow Wild River Road to the Wild River Campground. The Basin Trail leaves from the campground parking area.

This relatively easy hike takes you to the edge – the edge of a cirque. The trail begins along an old logging path, climbing more steeply during the second portion. As you near the lookout point, you'll pass a series of intersecting trails. Stay on the Basin Trail until it meets the Basin Rim Trail, and then go about .1 mile south for the view. The bowl that opens beneath you is the work of an alpine glacier, which scooped out one of the loveliest hollows in these mountains. At the bottom sits Basin Pond, a shiny treasure created not by the glacier but by damming. The sides of the bowl slope steeply to the water, spiked all around with deep green spruce and chunks of torn stone. *Note: You can also begin this hike from the other end, near Basin Pond. (See Steven Smith's Ponds and Lakes of the White Mountains.)*

Distance to lookout: 2.3 miles; time: 100 minutes.

South Baldface and Eastman Mountains
Directions: The trail leaves from the parking area off State 113, .1 mile north of the Appalachian Mountain Club's Cold River Camp.

Both of the Baldface peaks, North (3,591 feet) and South (3,569 feet), have, quite literally, bald faces. During a ferocious fire in 1903, which burned for a week, the two peaks were stripped of vegetation, exposing the remaining topsoil to erosion. The four miles of open rock that resulted provide some of the best views in the White Mountains — and some challenging climbing. The entire Baldface loop, which includes some tricky ledges, is not for first-time climbers. But at least there are several shorter alternatives.

The Slippery Brook Trail, which runs through the woods and across several brooks, reaches a junction at about 2.4 miles. From here, you can go left to Eastman Mountain (2,936 feet), a little-visited lower peak with great views of nearby South Baldface. Or you can go right on the Baldface Knob Trail to the summit of South Baldface. From there you can see Mount Washington, the rounded mass of Carter Dome, East and West Royce. (This route avoids the steep ledges on the Baldface Circle Trail.)

Distance from Slippery Brook Trail to Eastman Mountain: .8 mile; time: forty minutes. Distance from Slippery Brook Trail to South Baldface summit: .7 mile; time: thirty-five minutes.

WHITE MOUNTAINS NORTH

RANDOLPH AREA

Randolph is a virtually invisible town, tucked between the Crescent Range to the north and the northern peaks of the White Mountain National Forest to the south. Only two small signs along busy US 2 indicate the roads to Randolph, which actually has two distinct centers, each quiet street lined with cottages hidden in the trees. The peaks of Mount Madison and Mount Adams loom so close that the place feels as if it's been preserved in miniature, suspended in time beneath the towering shadows.

It was these mountains that first drew people to the Randolph area — and still draws them. The Randolph Mountain Club

(RMC), formed in 1910 to help rebuild and redesign the trails that had been lost to logging, is still active today, carrying on many Randolph traditions—weekly hikes, an annual mountain rendezvous, a club picnic. The RMC maintains four camps, open to the public for a small fee. And it publishes a useful guide and map to the region. Backpackers should consider as destinations Gray Knob Camp on Nowell Ridge and Crag Camp on the edge of King Ravine. *Note: Most of the trails in this area begin on private land—sometimes right at the end of someone's driveway. Please respect the privacy and rights of these property owners, who share these trails with the public.*

Contact the Randolph Mountain Club (RMC), Randolph, NH 03570; or the White Mountain National Forest Androscoggin Ranger Station, 80 Glen Road, Gorham, NH 03581; 603-466-2713.

Pine Mountain

Directions: From State 16 (near the Dolly Copp Campground), drive 1.9 miles on Pinkham B (Dolly Copp) Road to Pine Mountain Road. Leave your car in the parking area on the left and follow the private dirt road for one mile to the start of the very short Ledge Trail. Pine Mountain is also accessible from the other end of the Pinkham B Road, 2.4 miles from US 2.

Pine Mountain is the little guy at the very end of a long string of famous mountains. The only one of the Presidentials not named for a person, this 2,410-foot peak at the very northern tip of the range is tucked in low and close to its looming neighbors. Across its wide ledge of erosion-resistant schist is an unusually clear example of glacial striations—long, parallel scrape marks left by the glacier as it plowed over the mountains.

The trail to the summit begins with a mile of dirt-road walking, but the short, steep scramble up the Ledge Trail to the south ledges quickly brings you face-to-face with Mount Madison,

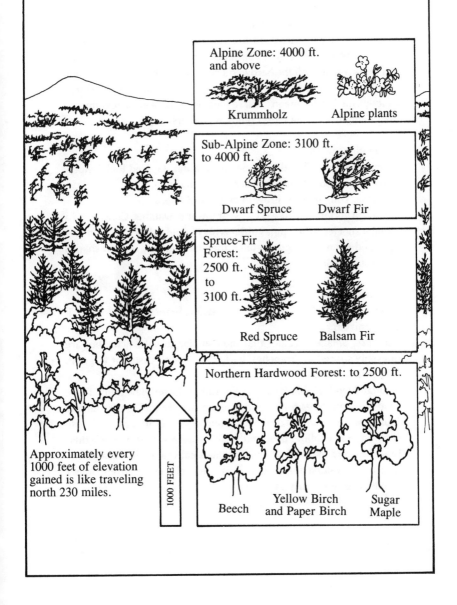

WHITE MOUNTAIN LAND ZONES

Alpine Zone: 4000 ft. and above

Krummholz   Alpine plants

Sub-Alpine Zone: 3100 ft. to 4000 ft.

Dwarf Spruce   Dwarf Fir

Spruce-Fir Forest: 2500 ft. to 3100 ft.

Red Spruce   Balsam Fir

Northern Hardwood Forest: to 2500 ft.

Beech   Yellow Birch and Paper Birch   Sugar Maple

Approximately every 1000 feet of elevation gained is like traveling north 230 miles.

1000 FEET

TREE TIPS

Prized for their lumber, conifers once covered most of New Hampshire's mountains; today, many of these peaks, heavily logged at the turn of the century, are covered with "second-growth" hardwood forests—trees that thrive on the full sunlight that floods cutover areas. As forest succession continues, shade-loving conifers gradually grow up beneath the hardwood canopy, until they dominate the forest once more. For those of you who have always wondered exactly which "evergreen" you're looking at, here are a few tips for identifying five of the most common conifers.

White Pine

From a distance: Broad branches have a flat, layered look; widely spaced; tree looks "rounded" across top and side.

Up close: Long needles grow in clusters of five.

Habitat: This familiar tree is found at lower elevations. Considered a pioneer species, white pines often grow in fields; they thrive on sunlight and cannot reproduce once they have grown up and shaded the ground below.

Hemlock

From a distance: Lacy, with slightly sagging branches that look a bit disorganized.

Up close: Smaller needles that look similar to balsam fir, but are unevenly spaced on branches; bark has purplish cast; not fragrant; very small cones.

Habitat: Hemlocks do well in moist soils at lower elevations. These shade-tolerant trees prefer to live along streams and are frequently found mixed in with hardwoods. Hemlocks are the most valuable softwood for wildlife: deer and ruffed grouse winter beneath their branches, and many birds and mammals eat the seeds. Because the tree is not valued for timber, it is often eliminated from timber stands; it is not nearly as common as balsam fir and red spruce in the White Mountain National Forest.

Balsam Fir
From a distance: Tall, slender, compact, and sharply pointed; blue-green color.
Up close: Smooth bark, branches in tiers, no nubs if you pull needles off. Two faint white stripes on undersides of needles, which are flat and soft and don't go all the way around the branch. Small cones are erect, instead of dangling below the branch. The quickest way to tell a fir from a spruce is to touch it: Fir feels soft; spruce feels sharp.
Habitat: These sweet-smelling trees take over at high elevations and, along with black spruce, can be found as *krummholz,* growing twisted and close to the ground above treeline.

Red Spruce
From a distance: Often grows mixed in with balsam fir, but can be distinguished by its more rounded top and looser, more "gaping" spaces between branches; color is more olive-green.
Up close: Scaly, lichen-covered bark. Needles are lighter green than balsam fir—and sharp; they fit tightly all the way around the branch; needles leave nubs if you pull them off.
Habitat: Red spruce covers the middle and higher elevations, usually mixed in with balsam fir. Black spruce, which, to the untrained eye, looks similar, is able to survive under harsher conditions and is often found with balsam fir as *krummholz,* the twisted trees that grow above treeline.

Tamarack (Larch)
From a distance: Droopy and "messy" looking, flimsy; almost web-like. Actually a deciduous tree, the tamarack loses its needles and often is mistaken for dead during the winter.
Up close: Light green needles are short and spiky, clustered in groups of twenty or thirty. They turn golden in the fall and drop in winter.
Habitat: Tamaracks, along with black spruce, can survive in nutrient-poor soil. Both are found at lower elevations, often in bogs, which are watery, but so nutrient-poor that very few species survive.

the peak of Mount Washington just visible behind. To the south and east, the horizon is a carved mass of mountain peaks, including Wildcat, Carter Dome, and the easy-to-spot rocky outcroppings of the Imp Profile. To the north, the great bend in the Androscoggin River glints against the green like a half-moon slice of silver.

Distance from Pinkham B Road to summit: 3.5 miles; time: two hours ten minutes.

Dome Rock

Directions: Trails begin just south of US 2, either from the Appalachia parking area or from Randolph East. Consult the *RMC Guide* for details.

Swept by fire in October 1921, Dome Rock (2,662 feet) sits smack in the middle of things, and you can too, if you make the short hike to its symmetrical bald summit. Two long, sharp ridges — Howker and Durand — rise to the east and west, and the Crescent Range spreads across the northern horizon. RMC member Doug Mayer recommends this ascent to Dome Rock: Begin at Appalachia along Fallsway and follow Valley Way and Brookside (two very short stretches) to the Inlook Trail, which takes you through Snyder Brook's old-growth forest (see box, page 124) and past waterfalls and open ledges en route to your destination.

Distance: 1.6 or 1.8 miles, depending on your approach; time: about ninety minutes.

Lookout Ledge

Directions: From US 2, turn onto Durand Road at Lowe's Store. Sargent Path begins about one mile down on the left, just after a red house.

You have to lean into the mountain along the steep, little-used Sargent Path that leads to Lookout Ledge (2,240 feet). This is the quickest — and steepest — way up. But it allows you to make a loop, returning on the more gradual Ledge Trail and then walking a short distance to your car along quiet Durand Road. For a much longer (plan on a day) and more scenic route, head up the Crescent Ridge Trail, across Mount Crescent (3,230 feet) and Mount Randolph (3,070 feet), and back down to Lookout Ledge. Either way you do it, you'll end up at the granite ledge with its wide-open view. The northern Presidentials stand huge and forbidding close in front of you, and the gray jumble of King Ravine, where Mount Madison and Mount Adams meet (see entry below), opens across the way like a gaping shadow, awesome and stark.

Distance: .8 mile; time: fifty minutes, via Sargent Path.

King Ravine

Directions: Trails begin at the Appalachia parking lot and across from Lowe's Store, both off US 2. See the *RMC Guide* for details.

Unitarian clergyman Thomas Starr King, the man for whom this ravine is named, described it as "the grandest of all gorges that have been cloven out of the White Hills." He praised its "deep divinity — the sweep of its keen-edged walls from the very shoulder of the mountain to its feet by the Randolph road." In his 1859 classic, *The White Hills,* he reflected on a visit to the ravine: "We sat some time . . . looking at the rocky desolation and horror. . . . The huge cone of Mt. Madison rose before us, steep, symmetrical, and sharp, with more commanding beauty of form than any other summit of the White Hills has ever shown to my eye. . . ."

King Ravine forms the deep fold between — and below — Mounts Madison and Adams. But you do have to climb to get there. And it's not easy, no matter how you choose to do it (King

Ravine Trail or Short Line). Says one hiker, "This is not most people's idea of hiking." The trail disappears among boulders as big as houses and slips past caves that harbor year-round ice. Geologists identify this "rocky desolation" as a fossil rock glacier that once slipped along on a sheet of leftover glacial ice on the bottom of this cirque (see box below). Today, this cold, shadowy

---

HAVE YOU EVER SEEN A FELSENMEER CREEP?

This is one of Brian Fowler's favorite questions. Fowler is president of the Mount Washington Observatory and a geologist who specializes in alpine glaciology. He is, in other words, a cirque enthusiast, a lover of those giant glacier-carved bowls that add their sculpted drama to the mountain landscape. Of the eight cirques in the White Mountains, King Ravine, one of the relatively accessible and most dramatic examples, is the third largest, after the Great Gulf and Castle Ravine. Tuckerman Ravine, the best-known glacial bowl, is the fifth largest. All of these cirques are the work of smaller alpine glaciers that remained in the hollows between periods of sheet glaciation.

King Ravine's tumble of boulders — known as a fossil rock glacier — is no longer active, but its mark is very much visible. The story begins about 10,000 years ago, just after the glacier retreated, a time when the climate was undergoing extreme temperature swings. These oscillating temperatures literally shattered the mountain peaks, creating piles of rubble. "If you've hiked the Presidential Ridge, you know what it looks like," says Fowler, "like somebody backed up a truck and dumped it there."

Eventually, much of that loose rock tumbled down into the cirque — on top of a leftover ice sheet that remained along the floor. It was this ice that transported the boulders, spreading them along the ravine as it crept. The rocky maze so intriguing to hikers today is, in fact, the result of a phenomenon known as *felsenmeer* creep. (*Felsenmeer* is the German word for "rock waves" or "sea of rocks.") The creeping ice beneath this rock glacier has long since melted, but the wave of rocks remains.

ravine is one of the best places in the mountains to look up at, instead of out from, the great summits. Study a map before you go, and get more information from the ranger station.

Distance: depending on your route and how far into the ravine you choose to go, the one-way trip could range from two to four miles and take anywhere from two to three hours.

The North Country

Not only for strength, but for beauty,
the poet must, from time to time, travel the logger's
path . . . to drink at some new and more
bracing fountain of the Muses, far in the recesses
of the wilderness.

— Henry David Thoreau, *The Maine Woods*

Something changes as you go north. Something to do with space
and distance. Something to do with land and sky and where they
meet. This is not the jagged edge and shadow of the White Mountains. The land here is more rolling, most of it forested, some of
it covered with working dairy farms. Along Hollow Road (State
145), the "back road" to Pittsburg, wide fields spread across deep
valleys, a landscape found nowhere else in New Hampshire.

Farther north, the forests close in. The land here lies within
New Hampshire borders, but it belongs, in spirit, to the twenty-
six-million-acre forest that stretches across northern New England from Maine to the Adirondacks. This expanse of spruce-fir
forest, about which Thoreau waxed so poetic, has changed since

1846, when he left Concord and headed north. Once known only to hunters and loggers, the forest has reached a crucial point in its history, as questions of land use become ever more complex. But you can still feel, as you drive north, the shifting balance. Cities, then towns and villages, seem to shrink against the landscape, and people are in the minority.

This chapter takes you north — from the southwestern corner just on the edge of the White Mountain National Forest to the rugged Mahoosuc Range; on to the forested slopes of the Kilkenny region and Nash Stream Valley; north to Lake Umbagog and Dixville Notch; and then, farther north still, to the four Connecticut Lakes and the trickle of water that marks the very start of the Connecticut River. It takes you as far north as you can possibly go, to a place where civilization seems puny, and there is only the land.

SOUTHWEST CORNER

From the stone fire tower on the top of Mount Prospect, it's hard to know which way to look: the White Mountains lie to the south, the ranges of the North Country to the north. The southwestern corner is, in a sense, where the transition between the two regions begins. The change is gradual, but when you have to look *south* to the White Mountains, you know you've begun your journey through the North Country.

Weeks State Park

This mountaintop historic site provides a glimpse into history and the life of the man who helped establish the White Mountain National Forest.

Directions: The park is 2.4 miles south of Lancaster, on US 3.

From the picture windows of the Weeks estate at the top of

Mount Prospect, it's clear why John Wingate Weeks (1860–1926) chose this spot for his summer retreat. The mountains that he loved — the Presidentials, the Kilkennys, the Percy Peaks — spread out in every direction, unfolding to the horizon in shifting shades of gray and blue. Weeks, who was born in Lancaster, is best known for the 1911 Weeks Law (see box, page 112), which forever changed the face of New Hampshire. "This is the ideal place to celebrate the founding of the White Mountain National Forest," says park manager Pat Nelson, "because you get a spectacular look at it."

The estate itself — which includes 420 acres of land on Mount Prospect (2,059 feet) — represents the conservation movement that was growing at the turn of the twentieth century. As less-profitable farms were abandoned, investors like Weeks bought and preserved the land. Inside, a display of black-and-white photographs tells the story of nineteenth-century logging in the New Hampshire mountains, an era that led, ironically, to the rescue of the forest. Outside, the stone fire tower offers even more expansive views.

A new three-mile trail around the base of the mountain, specially designed for cross-country skiing, makes good walking, too, through northern hardwood and spruce-fir forests. It includes a portion of the North-South Heritage Trail, which eventually will run the length of the state.

To do: *hiking, picnicking; scenic auto road; historic fire tower; house tours; forestry and conservation exhibits; mounted bird collection; evening programs in summer. Contact Weeks State Park Association, P.O. Box 104, Lancaster, NH 03574; 603-788-4004 (in-season); 603-788-3155 (off-season).*

The Rocks
This 1,300-acre North Country center for the Society for the Protection of New Hampshire Forests (Forest Society) includes

walking trails, a Christmas-tree farm, and educational activities year-round.

Directions: From I-93, take Exit 40 and drive .5 mile east on US 302 toward Bethlehem. Turn right onto Glessner Road and continue to the parking area.

Gentleman farmer John Glessner loved hay fields. When he built his estate in 1884, he situated the house on a hill overlooking rolling pastureland grazed by Jersey cattle. The house no longer exists, but the land — and the giant boulders for which the property is named — remain. Many of the fields have been reclaimed by forests, now owned and managed by the Forest Society. Trails lead past reseeded landings and areas that have been selectively harvested for minimal impact.

Along the Woodland Trail, watch for the little field in the woods near the old Sawmill-Pigpen, a sagging old structure with an unusual dual purpose. "People realize there's a little field in the woods," says property manager Nigel Manley, "but they don't know why." The idea is simple: Instead of creating many small areas in the woods where cut trees can be loaded onto trucks, a single larger area has been created, which can be used again when the area is logged in the future. Fewer trees are damaged this way, and once the landing area has been covered with topsoil and seeded, the small field provides habitat for wildlife.

Along the Return Loop Trail, selective cutting has created a different sort of forest: bright and open. The other tree business on this property, the Christmas-tree plantation, has its own trail, which winds among stretches of neatly planted, perfectly shaped little balsam firs. Here on the fields where cows once grazed, 7,000 seedlings are planted each year, then sheared and shaped for a decade until they are ready for harvesting.

Programs throughout the year at The Rocks focus on timber

and wildlife management. The guided walk during the June Wildflower Festival is the best time to spot one of the estate's hidden treasures: the rare yellow lady's slipper, one of many species of wildflowers introduced here by Mrs. Glessner.

To do: bird-watching, snowshoeing, cross-country skiing; walking trails (also open to horses); Christmas tree farm; educational programs. Contact The Rocks, RFD 1, Bethlehem, NH 02374; 603-444-6228; or contact SPNHF, 54 Portsmouth Street, Concord, NH 03301; 603-224-9945.

Bretzfelder Memorial Park

This small park, an easy side trip from The Rocks, has a tiny pond, a giant memorial pine tree, and an interpretive nature trail.

Directions: From I-93, take Exit 40 and drive east toward Bethlehem on US 302. Drive two miles and turn left onto Prospect Street, which is one mile north of Bethlehem village. Drive another mile and turn left into the park.

The giant memorial tree stands alone, at the center of a tiny, secluded grove. Stepping inside is like entering a piney chapel: The light dims and sound is silenced. At the foot of the towering white pine, a plaque commemorates the man who loved this land and came often to this spot, Charles B. Bretzfelder: "May his wisdom and his light forever grow upon this earth." The Four Seasons Trail that winds through this seventy-seven-acre park, much of which is managed for timber, was built by local sixth graders. The trail guide, also produced by sixth graders, teaches about, among other things, great blue herons, white pines, granite, and moose.

To do: bird-watching, fishing, cross-country skiing, snowshoeing, picnicking, skating; self-guided nature trail. Trail guides to the Four Seasons Trail are available at the trailhead. Contact The Rocks, RFD 1, Bethlehem, NH 02374; 603-444-6228.

Pondicherry
This 312-acre National Natural Landmark, with its two ponds and mountain backdrop, is considered one of the very best birding locations in New Hampshire.

Directions: From the dirt parking area at the Whitefield airport, drive an old railroad right-of-way to the end (about a mile), where it meets the railroad tracks. Follow the tracks .7 mile to the refuge.

In a canoe, out in the middle of Big Cherry Pond, you're completely surrounded. The northern Presidentials, the Twin and Franconia ranges, the Pliny Range – mountains loom on every side, and there's not a building in sight. Tudor Richards, longtime former director of the Audubon Society of New Hampshire (ASNH), calls this property "Audubon's most spectacular."

If you can take your eyes off the view, you'll find yourself in prime birding territory: Look for both of the rare three-toed woodpeckers – the black-backed and the northern – as well as pileated woodpeckers, gray jays, and boreal chickadees. On the water, watch for ring-necked ducks, wood ducks, black ducks, and the bright-colored wing patches that identify the blue-winged and green-winged teals. There's also a heron rookery here, and a resident pair of nesting loons.

The walk in to the refuge follows an old railroad bed (trains still pass once a day or so at slow speeds) for about thirty minutes. When the tracks fork left (look for the balsam poplar here, uncommon in New Hampshire), follow them to the edge of Big Cherry Pond, a 100-acre, bog-circled pond that is gradually filling in. "Come back in a couple thousand years," says Dave Govatski, ASNH land steward for this property, "and it'll be gone." Meanwhile, canoeists can put in here and walkers can settle in for some bird-watching. Near the pond, you might spot turtle eggs laid among the tracks.

If you crave greater remoteness, continue down the tracks for several yards, watching carefully for a trail that starts on the left. It's hard to find but is very clear once you do. Another twenty minutes of walking (which can be quite wet in spring) leads to thirty-acre Little Cherry Pond, hidden deep in the woods. Watch for moose tracks on the way in, and, as you near the pond, pitcher plants and other bog-loving flora that thrive in this environment. If you are paddling, make your way from Big Cherry to Little Cherry, slipping soundlessly past the boggy shores; then explore the winding backwaters of the Johns River, behind the smaller pond. (While you're in the area, you may also want to explore ASNH's smaller **Scotland Brook Sanctuary** in Sugar Hill.)

To do: bird-watching, canoeing (must portage along railroad tracks to the pond). Contact ASNH, 3 Silk Farm Road, Concord, NH 03301; 603-224-9909.

MAHOOSUC RANGE

Just north of the White Mountain National Forest, on the easternmost side of the state, the Mahoosuc Range stretches north and east from the great bend in the Androscoggin River, rising out of Berlin's and Gorham's industrial haze and on into Maine. Those who hike here love its lack of crowds, its rough and rugged terrain — and its stunning views. There are ponds to explore, including Gentian Pond, Dream Lake, and Page Pond — a trio of watery hollows strung along the Mahoosuc Trail. And there are bogs, which have formed in nearly every shallow depression left by the glacier. "The whole range," says one hiker, "feels like an inverted bog."

Contact the White Mountain National Forest Androscoggin Ranger Station, 80 Glen Road, Gorham, NH 03581; 603-466-2713.

Mascot Pond

Directions: From Gorham, drive .4 mile north on State 16. Pull off and park beneath the railroad bridge that crosses the river here. This is where the trail begins.

Yes, this is the start of the Mahoosuc Trail – along an old metal railroad bridge, just off a busy highway between two mill towns. Watch your head as you step onto the bridge, ducking low beneath two crossed iron girders. The boards vibrate underfoot

Long-eared bat

THE BATS OF MASCOT MINE

An awful lot of bats hang out in Mascot Mine — at last count, about 1,500. The abandoned mine is the biggest known hibernaculum in the state, winter home to five of the eight or nine bat species found in New Hampshire. A 1993 study conducted by The Nature Conservancy, which holds an easement on this state property, determined that 1,280 of the hibernators were little brown bats, the kind you might find in your attic. But there were also 127 long-eared bats, 86 big brown bats, two rare pipistrelles, and three of the state-endangered small-footed bats, hardly as long as your thumb.

"It's a good place for them," says The Nature Conservancy's Krista Helmboldt, because different bats need slightly different conditions for hibernation. We found them all over the shafts." Big brown bats, which can tolerate the cold, hang closer to the cave opening; others require more stable temperatures and hibernate deeper in the earth. Some species hang in clusters; others hang alone. Some hang high; others hang low. The metal gate erected across the face of Mascot Mine is designed to protect humans (the mine is quite deep) as well as the hibernators. If a bat is disturbed during the winter, it could lose ten to thirty days' worth of energy, which could mean death before summer.

Often mistaken for rodents, bats are actually the only species of flying mammals. They can live more than thirty years and spend most of their waking hours swooping through the air, consuming up to 3,000 insects a night. When temperatures start dropping, and their food supply dwindles, bats go in search of a winter residence. In a process called "swarming," they congregate by the hundreds in or near the mouths of caves before they enter and go into deep hibernation. During the winter, they maintain a body temperature cold enough to slow their metabolic rate, but not so cold that they freeze. They are the only mammals that can regulate their body temperature to this degree.

Unlike the softer limestone of Vermont, New Hampshire's bedrock, primarily composed of granite and schist, has few naturally occurring caves. None of the seven known hibernacula here are located in caves — all are in abandoned mines. Mascot Mine's south-facing exposure makes it an especially good wintering site. In summer, the bats head first for the pond, in search of water and food after their long winter, and then fly off to summer roosting spots: in tree crevices and bat houses, under eaves and in attics.

as you make this crossing – the rocky riverbed below, the railroad tracks overhead, the sound of traffic behind. Ahead, at the end of a dirt road and just before you reach the woods, you need to cross the top of a dam. The turbines churn below, generating power for the nearby James River Paper Mill, their throbbing bass eerie in the deserted stillness at the edge of the woods.

The short trail climbs steeply first, then levels out. After a mile, a short side trail departs to the pond, where you can spot giant Mount Madison just behind the curve of little Pine Mountain, an antenna poking from its wooded summit. Turn around and you'll spot the jagged gash of Leadmine Ledge, a rocky mess of shattered rock spilling down to the water's edge. For six years in the 1880s, the Mascot Mine Company blasted for lead here, shipping the ore to Boston. When the vein ran out, the mine was abandoned. Today the lower mine shaft houses New Hampshire's largest bat hibernaculum (see box, page 174).

Distance to Mascot Pond: 1.3 miles; time: about fifty minutes.

Mount Hayes

Directions: See directions for Mascot Pond. Cross the footbridge below the railroad bridge, follow the road to the right along the river .4 mile, and cross the canal. Continue 100 yards to the woods and the trail sign.

The beginning of the trail to Mount Hayes has the same landmarks as the trail to Mascot Pond – up and over the railroad bridge, across the top of the dam, and then into the woods. Instead of turning off for the pond, continue along the Mahoosuc Trail, which ascends through the woods, climbing steeply in spots, to ledges just below the summit. The view here stretches south toward the northern Presidentials and the Carter Range, with Pinkham Notch a deep valley in between. From the true summit, another half mile up, the view is to the north along the Androscoggin River and toward the other summits of the Mahoosuc Range.

Distance from State 16 to summit: 3.1 miles; time: two hours twenty minutes.

Mount Success

Directions: From Hutchins Street in Berlin, follow Success Pond Road 5.4 miles to the Success Trail. Watch carefully for the sign.

"If you climb Success (3,656 feet), you've got to make sure not to miss The Outlook," says Gene Daniell, editor of the *AMC Guide*. "It's much more interesting than the summit, and it gives you a comprehensive view of the North Country." Unlike the summit, which is so flat and broad that all the valleys are blocked from your field of vision, The Outlook, reached by a side loop about halfway up, hangs off the side of the mountain like a shelf. As you stand here, suspended in space, there's nothing but your own two feet between you and the deep, wide views below.

Distance: three miles; time: two hours thirty minutes.

Thirteen-Mile Woods

Directions: This scenic drive, just north of the Mahoosuc region, extends from Milan to Errol along State 16.

On a gray, drizzly day, raindrops dimple the surface of the winding Androscoggin River, pounding it like pewter. Once the scene of great log drives headed for Berlin and Gorham, the river is protected by a conservation easement on this paper-company land. The river winds wide and unspoiled close by the road, making it one of the loveliest scenic drives in New Hampshire. At Mollidgewock, a small public campground just off the road, canoeists sleep in campsites so near the water that they can roll out of their sleeping bags, into their canoes, and onto the river. Birders praise the birding, fishermen love the fishing. And the tales of moose sightings along this road are legendary. "Never driven it, no matter what time of day, without seeing one," says a local resident. What you won't see are buildings. Or billboards. Just the river.

KILKENNY REGION

It's easy to feel alone in the Kilkennys. The trails here are less trampled than many in the White Mountain National Forest, the stillness more absolute. The region has an emptiness about it, as if no one had discovered these woods. But, of course, they have. Like much of the state, this area was logged for spruce during the late 1800s. In 1903, massive forest fires consumed 25,000 acres, more than half the region. This land has grown in with acres of birch, open and light. Thick with ferns, it is almost parklike. And hikers who venture into these woods discover a solitude not found farther south.

Contact the White Mountain National Forest Androscoggin Ranger Station, 80 Glen Road, Gorham, NH 03581; 603-466-2713.

Devil's Hopyard

Directions: The Kilkenny Ridge Trail, which leads to the side trail to the Devil's Hopyard, begins at the South Pond Recreation Area (see page 178).

It's not hard to understand how this place got its name. The trail begins along a brook and winds through a hardwood forest of beech and sugar maple. But after a half mile or so, you round a bend, the land closes in on both sides, steep and angled, and you begin to have this spooky feeling that there's no way out. Ahead lies a jumbled mass of boulders, stretching to the end of a narrow, seventy-five-foot-wide gorge. The air is chill and damp, the light dim. In places, ice remains year-round. It feels — well, otherworldly.

A good example of stoss and lee topography (see box, page 132), this boulder-strewn ice gorge was left in the glacier's wake as it moved up and over the top, shattering the cliff and creating the rubble that eventually tumbled its way to the bottom of the ravine. Today, "stairstep moss" thrives in this shady, damp environment, growing in flattened emerald layers along every surface. Each "step" represents a year of growth. The red-spruce and balsam-fir needles scattered across this treacherous floor maintain the high acidity that encourages such lushness. Watch your step!

Distance from South Pond to Devil's Hopyard: 1.3 miles; time: fifty minutes.

South Pond

Directions: South Pond Recreation Area lies just off State 110 in Stark. *(**Note:** The access road to this area has a gate 1.1 miles from the pond. During summer, the gate is usually open from 9:00 A.M. to 8:00 P.M., but it's best to check with the ranger station for more information.)*

Plan a lakeside picnic. Take a dip in the cool waters. Paddle a canoe. Fish. This is a busy lake that makes room for motorboats, too. (The boat-launching ramp is not accessible by vehicle, so boats must be carried a short distance.) With luck, though, as you walk the trail along the lake's edge, beneath the hemlocks and birches, you'll hear only the loons that nest here. For a mountain view, trek to the south end of the pond and follow a short side spur left to catch a glimpse of Long Mountain (3,661 feet).

Note: South Pond is the starting point for hikes to the

Devil's Hopyard and Rogers Ledge. It also marks the northern terminus of the Kilkenny Ridge Trail.

Rogers Ledge
Directions: The Kilkenny Ridge Trail, which leads over Rogers Ledge, starts at South Pond.

Among those who love the Kilkenny region, Rogers Ledge is a favorite viewpoint. From the top, you can see east to the Mahoosucs, south to the Presidential Range, and straight down into the Kilkenny region itself. The steep southwest side of Rogers Ledge (2,945 feet) is nothing but a sheer cliff torn away by the glacier as it moved southward — rounding the north side, plucking the south side clean. A trip to this lookout could be easily combined with an excursion into the Devil's Hopyard or a picnic and swim at South Pond.

Distance from South Pond to Rogers Ledge: 4.1 miles; time: two hours fifty minutes.

Unknown Pond and the Horn
Directions: From Berlin, take State 110 to York Pond Road (on the left). Follow York Pond Road to the Berlin Fish Hatchery and then continue two miles west beyond the hatchery gate. Look for the Unknown Pond trailhead sign between a pond and a beaver swamp. (The gate is locked at 4:30 P.M. For more information, or to make arrangements to leave your car beyond the gate, call the fish hatchery: 603-449-3412.)

"Unknown Pond is one of the most remote yet accessible places in the mountains," says avid hiker Joe Gill, who works for the U.S. Forest Service and likes to look for the history hidden in the woods. As you walk here, watch carefully for the story of this second-growth forest. You are following an old railroad bed once used for removing timber from the woods. A grassy glen visible through the trees is the site of an old logging camp.

In one spot, giant pines, severed from their bases a century ago, lie rotting just off the trail, majestic even now. The stumps that remain grow nothing but torn fragments. Around these remnants, the hardwood forest sprouts in jumbled profusion – a crowd of deciduous trees and shrubs where there once stood only giant pines, widely spaced, with nothing below but darkness and soft needles.

The trail follows Unknown Pond Brook nearly all the way up through stands of birch until it reaches the pond itself, nestled amid a sweet fir forest. The solitude here, at the edge of this mountain pond, is complete. If you have the time and inclination, continue to the summit of the Horn (3,905 feet). From this rocky knob, considered the best peak in the region, you can look back at the pond and out at the endless forest.

Distance to Unknown Pond: 3.3 miles; time: two hours twenty minutes. Distance from Unknown Pond to the Horn: two miles; time: eighty-five minutes. (Side trail to the Horn is .3 mile and climbs 200+ feet.)

Kilkenny Ridge

Directions: The trail can be tackled from the north or the south. See the *AMC Guide* for details.

The Kilkenny Ridge Trail, which runs north to south for twenty miles along the Pilot–Pliny Ridge from South Pond to Mount Waumbek, makes a good three- or four-day trip for backpackers in search of a remote experience. "You can go for days up here without seeing anybody," says one forest ranger. Most of your trekking will be along old logging roads or railroad grades through second-growth forests. But the long tradition of logging continues here. From lookouts along the way, you're likely to see patches of lighter green or swatches of gray, evidence of timber harvesting.

NASH STREAM STATE FOREST

In 1988, the Nash Stream Forest was nearly lost. When Diamond International sold this land to Rancourt Associates, it looked as though years of timbering were about to be replaced by condominiums and vacation homes. The efforts of the Society for the Protection of New Hampshire Forests, The Nature Conservancy, and the state and federal governments saved 39,000 acres of the Nash Stream Valley. Much of the land on these primarily trailless summits is still managed for timber; some high-elevation areas have been designated as natural preserves, places where timbering is prohibited above 2,700 feet in an effort to save some rare plant species. From the summits of the Percy Peaks, accessible by trail, the views extend all the way south to the Presidentials, across a wide sea of green that remains unbroken by hacked-out patches of development.

Contact the New Hampshire Division of Forests and Lands, P.O. Box 856, Concord, NH 03302; 603-271-3456.

Percy Peaks

Directions: From State 110 in Groveton, go north on Emerson Road 2.2 miles and bear left on Nash Stream Road (gravel), which comes in on the left. Drive 2.7 miles to a parking area on the right. The trail starts fifty yards up the road.

North Percy (3,418 feet) and South Percy (3,220 feet) are the twin peaks of the North Country. Symmetrical and conical, they are the most conspicuous mountains in the northerly view from the top of Mount Washington. South Percy, which is wooded at the summit but has some good views, has no maintained trails.

But North Percy is bare except for low scrub, and the ascent, as one hiker describes it, is "steep but worth it." The first half of the trip follows the easy grades of an old logging road; the second half traverses several ledges that require hand- and footwork, each ledge offering an ever-wider view. Consult the *AMC Guide* for trail details.

Distance to summit of North Percy: 2.2 miles; time: two hours ten minutes.

Sugarloaf Mountain
Directions: Follow Nash Stream Road (see directions for Percy Peaks) 8.3 miles to a point sixty yards beyond its crossing with Nash Stream. Park in the grassy area.

On Sugarloaf, more remote than the Percy Peaks, the trail follows an old logging road that also served as the fire warden's trail when there was a fire tower at the summit. Running first through hardwoods, then through spruce and fir, the trail ascends steeply, the trees becoming shorter and shorter until they disappear on the exposed, rocky summit. From here, the Percy Peaks rise to the south and the whole Nash Stream Valley spreads out below.

Distance: 2.1 miles; time: two hours ten minutes.

LAKE UMBAGOG NATIONAL WILDLIFE REFUGE
New Hampshire's only pair of nesting eagles — and lots of other wildlife — find refuge on Lake Umbagog.

Directions: There are several convenient places to put in a canoe on Lake Umbagog — or Umbagog Lake, as locals call it. From Errol, on State 26, drive southeast 7.2 miles to the Umbagog Lake Campground, or .2 mile to the public boat-launching ramp on the upstream side of the Errol Dam on the Androscoggin

River. The put-in points closest to the lake's islands and wilderness campsites are north of town off State 16. Diamond Landing, an unimproved launching ramp on the Androscoggin River, is 1.6 miles north of Errol; Parson's Landing, on the Magalloway River, is 4.7 miles north of town. Ask for directions in Errol.

When an eagle wings across the sky, a fish dangling from its talons, you can almost hear the rush of air across feathers. Its wings beat in great, wide strokes, cutting across space and clouding the sky like some elemental force. The magnificent bird is headed straight for the top of a seventy-foot dead pine tree, back to two hungry eaglets. New Hampshire's only pair of nesting eagles live here on twelve-mile-long Lake Umbagog. Translated as "clear waters," *Umbagog* lives up to its Native American name: Its 7,850 acres of clear, shallow water make an ideal place for the birds to fish and raise their young.

"Umbagog is the richest wildlife habitat in the state," says Steve Breeser, manager of the Lake Umbagog National Wildlife Refuge. "It's probably the best example of undeveloped shoreline community we have." The newly formed refuge, still in the midst of land acquisition in 1993, eventually will include about 13,000 protected acres – the second-largest refuge in New England. "The key to a national wildlife refuge is the protection of habitat," explains Breeser. "Without habitat, there's nothing to manage." He reels off statistics about some of the creatures that thrive in these waters along with the eagles: 95 percent of the nesting osprey in the state; 15 percent of the loon population; lots of mink, otter, beaver, and muskrat; birds such as bitterns, rails, blue herons, kingfishers, thrushes, and twenty-five species of warblers. And of course there are moose.

The best way to experience Lake Umbagog is in a canoe, slipping silently through the water, watching. (Be sure to take binoculars and stay far enough away to avoid disturbing wildlife.) Explore the perimeter of Floating Island, a boggy mat covered with unusual vegetation. Paddle around Leonard Pond, where the Magalloway River flows into the lake and the Androscoggin River flows out. Camp at a secluded wilderness site on the edge of the lake or on an island. Sit on a rock and watch osprey carving spirals, their angled wings patterned white and black against the sky, their sharp eyes on the clear water below.

To do: wildlife watching, swimming, boating, camping, fishing, hunting. For information about the refuge, contact Lake Umbagog National Wildlife Refuge, Box 280, Errol, NH 03579. For information about camping, contact the Umbagog Lake Campground, P.O. Box 181, Errol, NH 03579; 603-482-7795.

Diamond Peaks

Directions: Drive nine miles north of Errol on State 16 until you reach Wentworths Location. Turn left at the dirt logging road just past the cemetery. Follow this road one mile and leave your car at the gatehouse. The trail up to the Diamond Peaks begins at the Management Center, 1.5 miles beyond the gate.

From the top of West Diamond Peak, the water below catches the late afternoon sun, winking like diamonds held to the light. Here, where the Swift Diamond and the Dead Diamond rivers become the Diamond River, the water cuts a deep gorge between Mount Dustan and the Diamond Peaks (2,071 feet) — and when the water is high, it provides an exhilarating, notoriously difficult run for kayakers. The two peaks, shoehorned in between the Diamond and Magalloway rivers, offer views from several ledges. Below lies the 26,900-acre Second College Grant, given to Dartmouth by the state in 1807.

Cabins on the property are available to those connected with Dartmouth and their guests; trails are open to all. On the road in, watch for the giant osprey nest high in a tree overlooking a broad marshy area — one of the oldest-known active nesting sites in the state. (You can call ahead to reserve a key for vehicle access, or you can park at the gate and walk 1.5 miles beyond the gate to the trailhead, stopping for a look at the gorge on the way. No camping or fires.)

Distance from the Management Center to East Diamond Peak: 1.1 miles; time: fifty-five minutes. Contact the gatekeeper: 603-482-3876; or contact Outdoor Programs, Dartmouth College, P.O. Box 9, Hanover, NH 03755.

DIXVILLE NOTCH

Most visitors to Dixville Notch are struck immediately by how much this jagged, wind-howling place differs from the notches farther south. The 1894 edition of Sweetser's *The White Mountains: A Handbook for Travelers* describes the notch as "a deep ravine among the hills whose impending cliffs are worn and broken into strange forms of ruin and desolation." Passing through the notch, Sweetser noted the "high and columnar sides . . . frowning at each other across the narrow chasm."

The difference, less poetically speaking, is in the rock. "The bedrock folded," says U.S. Geological Survey geologist Richard Moore, "turning the bedding and cleavage planes on end, so everything looks vertical." The schist, mixed with phyllite here, breaks off in sharp, flat planes, distinctly different from the bedrock found in the southern part of the state. W.C. Prime's description, included in Sweetser's book, wasn't very far from the geologic truth: "'. . . the Notch looks as if it had been produced by a convulsion of nature, which broke the mountain ridge from underneath, throwing the strata of rocks up into the air, and letting them fall in all directions. . . . Several pinnacles of rock, like the falling spires of cathedrals, stand out against the sky. . . .'"

The trails described below are on The Balsams hotel property, which also includes several miles of cross-country ski routes open for walking. For information and a trail guide, contact The

Balsams, Box 9, Dixville Notch, NH 03576; 800-255-0800 (in NH); 800-255-0600 (North America).

Table Rock

Directions: The short trail starts just off State 26, across the road from the entrance to The Balsams hotel; the long trail starts some 500 yards to the west, along State 26.

You're not quite standing on air when you're on top of Table Rock (2,720 feet). But almost. This is about the closest you can get to a bird's-eye view of Dixville Notch and still keep your feet on the ground. There are two ways up to this dizzying point: The easiest route leaves from the west trailhead, a short distance from the parking area. If you're looking for a steeper, fingertip-gripping climb, try the east route from the parking lot.

Distance from west trailhead: .7 mile; time: forty minutes. Distance from east trailhead near parking lot: .2 mile; time: thirty minutes.

Sanguinary Ridge

Directions: The trail starts just off State 26, at the end of Cold Spring Road, the entrance to The Balsams hotel.

Loose shards of rock and pebbles scatter underfoot as you climb to the first lookout point along Sanguinary Ridge (2,312 feet). This knife-edge climb weaves in tight switchbacks, rising quickly to an alpine zone, covered here and there with patches of mountain cranberry but littered mostly with loose rock. About halfway up, Pinnacle Rock stands alone, pointing a craggy finger to the sky. From the lookout point, the red-roofed turrets of the historic Balsams hotel below are bright against the emerald lawn, a pocket of civilization amid 15,000 acres of wilderness. Behind the hotel rises the sheer face of Abenaki Mountain, a nesting site for peregrine falcons (see box, facing page).

THE RETURN OF THE PEREGRINE FALCON
A pregrine falcon nest, almost invisible to the naked eye, sits high on Abenaki Mountain in Dixville Notch, perched on a virtually inaccessible cliff. Peregrines, best known for their diving ability, can hurtle downward toward their prey in a tight-winged "stoop" at speeds of more than 100 mph. But the sight of a peregrine streaking through the air is relatively rare in New Hampshire. As of 1993, this federally listed endangered bird nests at only eight sites in the state.

In the 1940s, about 350 breeding pairs of peregrines nested in cliffs east of the Mississippi River, including an estimated fifty-three pairs in Maine, New Hampshire, and Vermont. But then came DDT. With continued widespread use of this pesticide, contaminant levels in the bird's prey increased, and the females began laying thin-shelled eggs doomed never to hatch. By 1968, the peregrine was wiped out as a breeding species in the eastern United States. "Biologists were checking these cliff sites, where they knew peregrines had been in the past," says Chris Martin of the Audubon Society of New Hampshire. "At site after site, they were finding nothing. That was the real wake-up call on the whole issue of pesticides."

Use of DDT in the United States was finally banned in 1972 (although it continues to be manufactured by U.S. firms for sale abroad). The Peregrine Fund, established in 1970 at Cornell University, developed techniques for propagating young falcons in captivity and reintroducing them to the wild through a process called "hacking." Ninety-eight falcon chicks were released at Owls Head and Square Mountain in New Hampshire between 1976 and 1987. Overall, more than 4,000 peregrines have been hatched in captivity and released into the wild in at least thirty-six states and in Canada.

In 1981, a pair of peregrines discovered in New Hampshire's Franconia Notch became the first in almost three decades to raise young successfully on a natural cliff site anywhere in the eastern United States. Today the recovery effort and the study of these endangered raptors, which involves many organizations and individuals, continues. Using high-powered spotting scopes, field biologists and volunteer nest observers keep an eye on falcon "aeries," recording what they see. Accompanied by highly skilled rock climbers, biologists visit nearly inaccessible cliff-face aeries, banding young falcons at successful nests and retrieving important information from failed nests.

While the number of young produced and successfully raised fluctuates from year to year, there has been a slow but steady increase in the number of reoccupied territories. "The population in New England is almost to the point now where it could be downlisted," says White Mountain National Forest wildlife biologist John Lanier, who initiated New Hampshire's peregrine restoration program. "In 1980, just thirteen years ago, there were none. So, on a regional basis, it's a real success story."

From here, the trail follows the ridge in a steady downhill stretch, with views into Dixville Notch and south to the Mahoosuc Range. Part of the way, you're treading an old 1920s trail which ends at the Dixville Notch State Wayside area, amidst the sound of rushing water. The Flume here and Huntington Cascades across the street are both worth a look.

Return to the trailhead, walking with care, along State 26. A new trail, scheduled to open in the summer of 1994, will allow hikers to do a five-mile loop along Sanguinary Ridge on the northern side of the notch, down to the Flume, across to Huntington Cascades, and up along the southern ridge to Table Rock.

Distance along Sanguinary Ridge: 1.5 miles; time: ninety minutes.

CONNECTICUT LAKES REGION

This is as far as you can go. The one paved road here, US 3, runs straight through Pittsburg, New Hampshire's northernmost town, and on into Canada. Once claimed by both Canada and the United States, Pittsburg settled the dispute by declaring itself independent in 1832 as the Republic of Indian Stream. The republic wrote its own constitution, maintained a standing army, and survived, defiant, for three years, until the Indian Stream War – one short skirmish that led, eventually, to U.S. occupation. But the spirit of independence is still felt around here.

The town of Pittsburg (pop. 940) sprawls across 190,000 heavily forested acres – about six times the size of the average New Hampshire town. Here in the biggest township east of the Mississippi, most of the land is privately owned commercial forest (see page xxv). Narrow gravel roads cut through this paper-company property and must be used to reach some of the places listed below. Remember that logging trucks have the right-of-way here. Be alert for oncoming vehicles, and drive with extreme care. (Roads are generally not maintained in winter. No camping, fires, or ATVs.)

Contact New Hampshire's Connecticut Lakes Region, P.O. Box 400, Pittsburg, NH 03592; 603-538-7118. Roads and Trails of the Connecticut Lakes Region (designed for snowmobilers) is the most frequently used map of the area; USGS topographic maps are also available. Both are on sale in local stores. Be sure to ask for directions from local residents before you head out. Where to camp: Lake Francis State Park, Box 37B, River Road, Pittsburg, NH 03592; 603-538-6965. Deer Mountain Campground in the Connecticut Lakes States Forest, Pittsburg, NH 03592; 603-538-6965.

Scott Bog and East Inlet
Directions: From the U.S. Customs Station on the Canadian border, drive south on US 3 and take the first left after Deer Mountain Campground onto a gravel road. Cross the wooden bridge and bear left for Scott Bog, right for East Inlet. (The roads generally are closed during mud season, March 15 to May 30, and they are not maintained in winter.)

The best way to see Scott Bog or East Inlet is to take to the water – quietly. On an early morning canoe trip, the mist shifts and settles on the water. Pointed firs cut a spiky silhouette against a pink-and-blue sky. And wildlife is everywhere. Go softly here, through this stillness, and watch – for otter, mink, beaver, and

---

MOOSE: THE NORTH COUNTRY'S "TWIG-EATERS"

"Eater of twigs," the translation of the Algonquin word *moose*, seems an oddly diminutive description for so large and lumbering an animal. There's no question about it, moose are big: Males can grow to around six feet tall and weigh up to 1,400 pounds. The largest known moose antlers were measured at eighty-one inches across. Their ungainly gait comes from having front legs that are longer than back legs, an adaptation that makes it easier to jump over fallen trees. Despite their long-faced, homely appearance, these creatures are somehow both grand and lovable, and they thrive in the North Country, especially the Connecticut Lakes region.

It wasn't always this way. By 1850, unregulated hunting had nearly eliminated the moose. Finally, in 1901, the hunting season was closed in New Hampshire, but even as recently as 1950, the entire state population was estimated at only fifty. By 1988, the figure was up to 4,100, and today the population is thriving. The increase in the number of beaver, also nearly eliminated around the turn of the twentieth century, is one important reason for the return of the moose, which love the aquatic vegetation that grows along the edges of ponds – many of which have been created by beaver dams. Moose have been known to dive up to eighteen feet in search of the choicest morsels. Of course, they are also "eaters of twigs," especially in winter, when they survive on, among other things, hobblebush, striped maple (also called moosewood), poplar, and gray and white birch.

Route 3 north of Pittsburg is such a good area for spotting moose, especially at dusk, that it's known as Moose Alley. The animals are attracted to muddy swales in depressions along roadsides, where vegetation is salty from winter roadwork. Drive slowly. They tend to trot right across the road, and a moose-car collision can be serious. Moose are usually docile, but it's best to observe them from your car to avoid disturbing them.

Maybe you'll meet a moose

moose, especially in Moose Pasture Bog. Birders come here in search of the rare black-backed woodpecker. You might also spot the common snipe, ring-necked ducks, black ducks, mergansers, spruce grouse, Canada jays, boreal chickadees, and many species of warblers. Watch, too, for the fluttering hoary comma butterfly; its mottled black, white, and rust-colored wings are a rare sight in New Hampshire.

Although it's not visible from the water, the 426-acre parcel of land along East Inlet, donated by the Champion International paper company in 1987, includes one of the last low-elevation virgin spruce-fir stands in New Hampshire. These trees have never been timbered, but a spruce-budworm infestation that lasted from 1974 to 1982 killed many of the trees, so much of the forest is new growth. "What's unique about this forest," says Krista Helmboldt of The Nature Conservancy, "is it's never been subject to timber management – ever. Anything that has happened here has happened naturally." (See box, page 124.)

Contact The Nature Conservancy, 2½ Beacon Street, Suite 6, Concord, NH 03301; 603-224-5853. For road conditions, contact Champion International: 603-246-3331.

Magalloway Mountain

Directions: From the dam on First Connecticut Lake, follow US 3 north 4.7 miles and turn right onto Magalloway Mountain Road. (Watch for oncoming logging trucks along this road.) Drive 1.2 miles to a bridge across the Connecticut River. Take the right fork and continue to a fork at 2.3 miles. Bear left here and again at 2.9 miles. Turn right at 5.3 miles (watch for signs to the fire tower) and again at 6.3 miles. At 8.3 miles from US 3, the good road ends in a clearing. Park here and follow the warden's trail to the summit.

The northern forest is big. To understand just how big it is, climb the steep, loose-gravel trail to the wooded summit of

Magalloway Mountain (3,360 feet). Pause to catch your breath, and then climb the seventy steep, narrow stairs to the top of the fire tower. Below you is the forest – acres and acres of spiky fir and rounded spruce, textured green hills patterned with cloud-shadows. This is working forest, and large patches have been harvested – some by selective cutting, others by clear-cutting. Some patches are gray, freshly cut. Others are light green as the forest begins to grow back. The only visible road is the meandering logging route that cuts through the forest like a dry brown riverbed. The 360-degree view includes the Connecticut Lakes, Rump Mountain in Maine, and the Middle Branch of the Dead Diamond River. Don't miss the great view from the ledge just below the summit, behind the warden's cabin.

Distance from end of good road to fire tower: .8 mile; time: fifty minutes.

Garfield Falls

Directions: Access to Garfield Falls is along the Magalloway Road (see Magalloway Mountain directions). Instead of turning off at the fire-tower sign (5.3 miles from US 3), continue along Magalloway Road and watch for Paradise Camp on the left. About two miles beyond the camp, bear to the right where the road splits left and straight ahead. In another 1.1 miles, where the road makes a sharp left turn and crosses a bridge, continue straight ahead. In another 1.1 miles, you'll come to an open log yard with parking room on both sides of the road. The trail starts by a tree on the right side of the clearing on the left side of the road.

It's only a short walk to Garfield Falls – once you get there. The long drive is worth it, though. The five- or ten-minute walk to the falls passes through a quiet, pine-needled balsam forest, shaken by a faint rumbling. Suddenly the land drops away on your left and the rumbling bursts into a roar. The falls gush out from between two rocks with what seems an impossible force, the huge flow pounding out depressions in the boulders below and spinning into ferocious, rock-carving whirlpools. For the best view, clamber onto the huge boulder just downriver from the falls. Then dip your feet in the clear, cold water.

Fourth Connecticut Lake
Directions: Follow US 3 until you reach the Canadian border. Park at the U.S. Customs station, sign in, and pick up a map. The trail begins right behind the building.

There's something solemn about this place. Maybe it's the dark, enveloping silence of a spruce-fir forest — slender, lichen-covered trunks rising straight up on all sides, dead trees blown down across the forest floor, needles and moss thick along the ground. Maybe it's simply that you are here, at the very beginning, at the headwaters of the great Connecticut River. Fourth Connecticut Lake is more of a pond, really — two acres of water surrounded by four acres of floating peat bog, surrounded by forest. Champion International donated this seventy-eight-acre parcel of land to The Nature Conservancy in 1991. The hike in, steep and overgrown, follows the U.S.–Canada border, a wide swath of cut forest. Tread carefully along the water's edge looking for buckbean, pitcher plants, and other bog plants. And see if you can spot the trickle of water that is the river's source.

Distance: .5 mile; time: forty minutes. Contact The Nature Conservancy, 2½ Beacon Street, Suite 6, Concord, NH 03301; 603-224-5853.

Appendix

FOR MORE INFORMATION

"Green Organizations" in New Hampshire

Audubon Society
of New Hampshire
3 Silk Farm Road
Concord, NH 03301
603-224-9909

Great Bay Watch
Kingman Farm/UNH
Sea Grant Extension
Durham, NH 03824
603-749-1565

Lakes Region
Conservation Trust
P.O. Box 1097
Meredith, NH 03253
603-279-7278

Monadnock
Greenway Project
c/o *Monadnock Perspectives*
P.O. Box 95
West Peterborough, NH
03468
603-924-9114

The Nature Conservancy
2 ½ Beacon Street, Suite 6
Concord, NH 03301
603-224-5853

Society for the Protection of
New Hampshire Forests
54 Portsmouth Street
Concord, NH 03301
603-224-9945

Squam Lakes Association
P.O. Box 204
Holderness, NH 03245
603-968-7336

Squam Lakes
Conservation Society
P.O. Box 796
Meredith, NH 03253
603-279-1309

State and Federal Offices and Organizations

National Park Service
Saint-Gaudens National
Historic Site
Route 12A
Cornish, NH 03745
603-675-2175

New Hampshire Division of
Forests and Lands
P.O. Box 856
Concord, NH 03302
603-271-3456

New Hampshire Division of
Parks and Recreation
P.O. Box 856
Concord, NH 03302
603-271-3254

New Hampshire
Fish and Game Department
2 Hazen Drive
Concord, NH 03301
603-271-3421

New Hampshire Natural
Heritage Inventory Program
P.O. Box 856
Concord, NH 03302
603-271-3623

U.S. Fish and Wildlife
Service
22 Bridge Street, Unit 1
Concord, NH 03301
603-225-1411

White Mountain National Forest
719 Main Street, P.O. Box 638
Laconia, NH 03246
603-528-9528

EDUCATIONAL CENTERS

Amoskeag Fishway
c/o Public Service Company
of New Hampshire
1000 Elm Street,
P.O. Box 330
Manchester, NH 03105
603-634-2336
(or 603-626-FISH, in-season)

Harris Center for
Conservation Education
King's Highway
Hancock, NH 03449
603-525-3394

John Hay
National Wildlife Refuge
c/o New Hampshire Division
of Parks and Recreation
P.O. Box 856
Concord, NH 03302
603-271-3254

Merrimack River
Outdoor Education Area
and Conservation Center
Society for the Protection of
New Hampshire Forests
54 Portsmouth Street
Concord, NH 03301
603-224-9945

Paradise Point Nature Center
North Shore Road
East Hebron, NH 03232
603-744-3516

The Rocks
RFD 1
Bethlehem, NH 02374
603-444-6228

Sandy Point
Interpretive Center
c/o New Hampshire Fish
and Game Department
225 Main Street
Durham, NH 03824
603-868-1095

Science Center
of New Hampshire
P.O. Box 173
Holderness, NH 03245
603-968-7194

Seacoast Science Center
P.O. Box 674
Rye, NH 03870
603-436-8043

Silk Farm Wildlife Sanctuary
and Audubon Center
Audubon Society
of New Hampshire
3 Silk Farm Road
Concord, NH 03301
603-224-9909

University of New Hampshire
Cooperative Extension
110 Pettee Hall
University of New Hampshire
Durham, NH 03824
603-862-3591

Urban Forestry Center
45 Elwyn Road
Portsmouth, NH 03801
603-431-6774

MAPS, GUIDES, AND BOOKS
Many of the walks in this book follow clearly marked simple
loops through sanctuaries and preserved land. Be sure to pick up
the educational trail guides available at many of these trailheads.
Other places, especially those mentioned in the mountain regions
of the state, would be best undertaken with a map. See page xxiii
for information on other preparations you should make before
you go.

The AMC Hut System. A folder describing the huts operated
by the AMC for hikers; includes panoramic map of White
Mountains. Appalachian Mountain Club, 5 Joy Street, Boston,
MA 02108.

AMC White Mountain Guide. Detailed descriptions of trails in the White Mountains and other New Hampshire ranges. Appalachian Mountain Club, 5 Joy Street, Boston, MA 02108.

Dartmouth Outing Guide. Guide to trails in the Dartmouth region, Mount Moosilauke, Second College Grant (also eastern Vermont). Dartmouth Outing Club, Box 9, Hanover, NH 03755.

DeLorme's Trail Map & Guide to the White Mountain National Forest. Gives you the entire White Mountain National Forest at a glance; includes brief trail descriptions on back. DeLorme Mapping Company, P.O. Box 298, Freeport, ME 04032.

Fifty Hikes in the White Mountains, Daniel Doan. Hiking and backpacking trips in the high-peaks region of New Hampshire. Backcountry Publications, Woodstock, VT 05091.

Fifty More Hikes in New Hampshire, Daniel Doan. Day hikes and backpacking trips from Mount Monadnock to King Ravine. Backcountry Publications, Woodstock, VT 05091.

Guide to the Appalachian Trail in New Hampshire and Vermont. Appalachian Trail Conference, Box 807, Harpers Ferry, WV 25425.

Hiking Trails in Waterville Valley. Waterville Valley Athletic and Improvement Association map available at the Jugtown Country Store in Waterville, or from the town offices.

Metacomet-Monadnock Trail Guide. Guide to the M-and-M Trail from Massachusetts to Mount Monadnock, New Hampshire. Walter Banfield, RFD 3, Pratt Corner Road, Amherst, MA 01002.

Monadnock-Sunapee Greenway Trail Guide. SPNHF, 54 Portsmouth Street, Concord, NH 03301.

Mt. Monadnock. Five-color contour trail map. New England Cartographics, P.O. Box 9369, North Amherst, MA 01059.

Ponds and Lakes of the White Mountains, Steven D. Smith. Comprehensive guide for those who love to come upon water in the mountains. Backcountry Publications, Woodstock, VT 05091.

Randolph Valley and the Northern Peaks. Contour map. Mrs. D. E. Wilson, Randolph, NH 03570.

Sandwich Range Area. Map. Wonalancet Outdoor Club, Wonalancet, NH 03897.

Squam Trail Guide. Small guide to a few popular trails in the Squam Lakes area. Squam Lakes Association, P.O. Box 204, Holderness, NH 03245; 603-968-7336.

State map. New Hampshire Office of Travel and Tourism Development, P.O. Box 856, Concord, NH 03302-0856; 603-271-343. For statewide information, travel planner, highway map, and winter vacation information.

Wapack Trail Guide and Maps. Friends of the Wapack, P.O. Box 115, West Peterborough, NH 03468.

White Mountain National Forest. General recreation map with basic information for visitors. U.S. Forest Service, P.O. Box 638, Laconia, NH 03246.

White Mountain National Forest. The standard administrative map used by the Forest Service; more detailed than the visitor map. U.S. Forest Service, P.O. Box 638, Laconia, NH 03246.

Waterfalls of the White Mountains, Bruce and Doreen Bolnick. Backcountry Publications, Woodstock, VT 05091.

USGS topographic quadrangle maps. USGS has maps covering most of New Hampshire. An index showing map locations, ordering information, and local dealers is available. Branch of Distribution, U.S. Geological Survey, Box 25286, Federal Center, Denver, CO 80225.

AMC/Washburn Mount Washington and Presidential Range Map (AMC). Best available map of Presidential Range. AMC, Pinkham Notch Camp, P.O. Box 298, Pinkham Notch, NH 03581.

Index

Adams Point, 2–5
Algonquin Indians, 30
Allen's Ledge, 122
Amoskeag Dam, 56
Amoskeag Fishway, 55–56
ANIMALS
  bats, 74, 173, 174
  bears, 42, 45, 47, 62, 74, 85,
    95, 96, 97
  beavers, 45, 47, 52, 62, 80, 84,
    118, 137, 140, 155, 179,
    183, 190
  bobcats, 42, 43, 44, 74
  cats, 65
  coyotes, 7, 44, 74, 96
  deer, 7, 44, 47, 74, 76, 78, 85,
    96, 155, 160
  fishers, 42, 96
  foxes, 7, 74, 85
  hares, snowshoe, 44
  lynx, 44
  minks, 76, 183, 190
  moose, 42, 45, 47, 62, 76, 84,
    85, 96, 155, 170, 172, 177,
    183, 190, 191
  otters, 69, 73, 85, 96, 183, 190
  raccoons, 7, 65, 106
  reptiles, 74
  skunks, 7, 65

  squirrels, red, 92
  turtles, 51, 73, 75, 76, 108, 171
  weasels, 85
  wolves, 30
Archery range, 63
Artist Falls Brook, 152
Artist's Bluff, 134

Backpacking, 158, 180
Bacon Ledge, 46
Balsams, the, 185–186
Basin, the, 134, 136, 156
BEACHES
  on Big Squam Lake, 69, 70, 72
  Hampton Beach, 14
  on Lake Sunapee, 98
  on Star Island, 17
  Weirs Beach, 74
  on White Lake, 86
Bear Notch, 120, 121
Bickford Heights, 85
Big Deer Hill, 155
Bigelow Lawn, 133
Big Rock Cave, 114
BIKING
  Franconia Bike Path, 137
  in Odiorne Point State Park, 13

in Pillsbury State Park, 96
BIRDS
  bitterns, 183
  blackbirds, redwing, 5, 84
  bluebirds, 24, 51
  bluejays, 65
  buntings, 7, 14, 51, 64, 106
  chickadees, 24, 171, 192
  cormorants, double-crested, 17
  cowbirds, 65
  crossbills, gypsy, 84
  ducks, 14, 25, 28, 29, 32, 53,
      68, 69, 109, 151, 155, 171,
      192
  eagles, 2, 3, 4, 6, 57, 108, 182,
      183
  egrets, 4, 13, 17
  falcons, peregrine, 7, 57, 186,
      187
  flickers, 2, 24, 25
  flycatchers, 53, 64, 65
  gannets, 14
  geese, Canada, 4–5, 24
  gnatcatchers, blue-gray, 64
  goshawks, 64
  grebes, 14, 109
  grosbeaks, 25, 37, 51, 52
  grouse, 23, 25, 41, 78, 130–131,
      160, 192
  guillemot, black, 17
  gulls, 14, 15, 17
  harriers, 6, 7, 96, 109, 154
  hawks, 7, 26, 37, 38, 45, 78,
      84, 100
  herons, 2, 6, 9, 13, 23, 25, 40,
      68, 69, 79, 80–81, 83, 96,
      155, 170, 171, 183
  hummingbirds, 64, 108

ibis, glossy, 3, 17
jays, 171, 192
kestrels, 7
kingbirds, 84
kingfishers, 4, 68, 69, 70, 84,
    151, 183
kittiwakes, black-legged, 14
larks, horned, 14
loons, 7, 14, 24, 32, 69, 74, 76,
    77, 96, 107, 151, 171, 178,
    183
oldsquaw, 14
orioles, 51, 64
orioles, Baltimore, 51
ospreys, 6, 7, 96, 109, 183, 184
ovenbirds, 24, 65, 96
owls, barred, 7, 14, 24, 25, 58,
    59, 73, 108
petrels, 11
pewee, eastern wood, 81
plovers, 9, 13
rails, 183
redstarts, 96
robins, 24
sandpipers, 9, 13
sapsuckers, yellow-bellied, 78,
    95
scooters, white-winged, 14
shearwaters, 11
snipes, common, 192
sparrows, 24, 37
swallows, 64
tanagers, 7, 24, 51, 64
teals, 69, 171
terns, common, 7, 13
thrushes, 24, 25, 37, 64, 71, 99,
    106, 183
titmouse, tufted, 24

turkeys, wild, 7, 47
vireos, 64, 65, 96
vultures, turkey, 64
warblers, 7, 23, 24, 37, 58, 64,
    65, 68, 69, 71, 81, 96, 183,
    192
waterthrush, northern, 84
waxwings, cedar, 24, 37, 99,
    151
woodcock, American, 23, 24
woodpeckers, 23, 24, 75, 82,
    83, 95, 124, 151, 171
wrens, winter, 37, 80
yellowlegs, 13, 25
BIRD-WATCHING
along the Bellamy River, 25
at Bretzfelder Memorial Park,
    170
along the coast, 14
in Deering Wildlife Sanctuary,
    53
at Dixville and Franconia
    notches, 187–188
at Foss Farm, 24
on Great Bay, 2, 5, 6, 24
at Hebron Marsh Wildlife
    Sanctuary, 109
at Hoyt Wildlife Sanctuary, 83
at Knight's Pond, 81
at Meetinghouse Pond, 28, 29,
at Paradise Point Nature Center,
    108
in Pawtuckaway State Park, 64
at Pondicherry Refuge, 171, 172
at The Rocks, 170,
at Sagamore Creek, 23
at Scott Bog, 190, 192
on the South Woods Trail, 34

on Star Island, 17
at Stonedam Island Natural
    Area, 76
at Thirteen-Mile Woods, 177
at Thompson Bird Sanctuary, 83,
    84
at Lake Umbagog National
    Wildlife Refuge, 183, 184
in Unsworth Preserve, 68, 69
on a whale-watching cruise, 11
Black Spruce Ponds Preserve, 86
Blueberrying, 31, 32, 33, 34, 72
BOATING/CANOEING
in Bear Brook State Park, 62, 63
on Big Cherry Pond, 117
on Big Squam Lake, 70, 71, 72
on Chocorua Lake, 85
on the Diamond River, 184
on Meetinghouse Pond, 28, 29
on Mountain Pond, 151
in Northwood Meadows Pioneer
    Park, 66
in Pillsbury State Park, 96
on Pisgah Reservoir, 34
on Scott Bog, 189
in South Pond Recreation Area,
    178
on Lake Umbagog, 182, 183–184
in Unsworth Preserve, 69
on Upper Hall Pond, 117
whale-watching cruises, 9–12
on White Lake, 86, 87
BOGS
bog environment, 102
Cloudland Bog, 130
Deer Hill Bog, 155
Heath Pond Bog, 87
Moose Pasture Bog, 190

Mud Pond Bog, 53
Philbrick-Cricenti Bog, 100–101
Ponemah Bog, 49, 50–51
Scott Bog, 189–192
Smith Pond Bog, 51, 59
Boott Spur, 147
Bridge of Sighs, 143
Butterflies, 49–50, 57, 192

CAMPING/CAMPGROUNDS
   in Bear Brook State Park, 63
   near Big Squam Lake, 69, 70, 71
   Deer Mountain Campground,
      189
   Dolly Copp Campground, 147,
      158
   Lafayette Campground, 135, 136
   in Lake Francis State Park, 189
   Mollidgewock Campground, 176
   in Monadnock State Park, 30
   Passaconaway Campground, 121
   in Pawtuckaway State Park, 63,
      64
   in Pillsbury State Park, 96
   Umbagog Lake Campground,
      182, 184
   in White Lake State Park, 87
   in White Mountain National
      Forest, 113
   Wild River Campground, 156
   Zealand Campground, 127,
      128–129
Cannon Mountain Ski Area, 137
Canoeing. See Boating
Caps Ridge, 128
Carter Ledge, 118

Carter Notch, 149
Cathedral Ledge, 133, 153
Caves, bat, 174, 175
Caves in Lost River Gorge,
      142–143
Chairlift rides, 99
CITIES/TOWNS
   Allenstown, 62
   Alton, 79
   Amherst, 49, 50
   Antrim, 41
   Bartlett, 131
   Benton, 139
   Berlin, 48, 172, 176, 179
   Bethel, 154
   Bethlehem, 125, 135, 169, 170
   Bristol, 107
   Campton, 115
   Canaan, 106
   Center Harbor, 69, 72
   Center Sandwich, 114, 115
   Chesterfield, 34
   Chocorua, 85, 86
   Colebrook, 189
   Concord, 29, 33, 38, 40, 41, 46,
      48, 49, 55, 59, 60, 61, 62,
      66, 83, 84, 86, 89, 95, 98,
      107, 170, 172, 181, 192, 194
   Conway, 48, 81, 113, 120, 121
   Cornish, 103, 104, 105, 106
   Crawford Notch, 125
   Derry, 54, 55
   Dixville Notch, 186
   Dover, 25
   Dublin, 29
   Durham, 2, 6, 24, 25
   East Haverhill, 139
   East Hebron, 107, 108

Effingham Falls, 81
Errol, 176, 182, 183, 184
Fitzwilliam, 35
Freedom, 87
Gilford, 77, 78
Glen, 154
Gorham, 146, 158, 172, 173, 177
Greenfield, 36, 37
Groveton, 181
Hampton, 18
Hancock, 31, 38, 42, 45
Hanover, 185
Hebron, 108
Hillsborough, 51, 53, 54
Hinsdale, 34
Holderness, 70, 71, 73, 74
Hookset, 62
Hopkinton, 51, 58
Intervale, 150, 151
Jaffrey, 27, 29, 30, 32, 35, 98
Keene, 48
Laconia, 74, 78
Lancaster, 112, 167, 168
Lincoln, 120, 135, 137
Littleton, 48
Madison, 86
Manchester, 49, 55, 56
Meredith, 69, 76, 81
Meriden, 105
Milan, 176
Moultonborough, 77
Newbury, 91, 94, 95, 96, 98
New London, 100, 101
North Conway, 133, 149, 150,
    152, 154
North Hampton, 19
North Haverhill, 139
North Sandwich, 84

North Sutton, 100
Northwood, 64
North Woodstock, 135, 138, 141,
    142, 144
Peterborough, 35, 36, 39
Pittsburg, 166, 188, 189, 190
Plymouth, 117
Portsmouth, 6, 7, 9, 12, 16, 17,
    18, 19, 22
Randolph, 157, 158, 162
Raymond, 63, 64
Rochester, 26
Rye, 9, 12, 18
Sandwich, 117
South Chatham, 150
South Tamworth, 84
Stark, 178
Stoddard, 31, 45
Stowe, 155
Stratham, 5
Suncook, 63
Tamworth, 86
Warner, 99
Warren, 140
Washington, 95, 96
Waterville, 117
Wentworths Location, 184
West Ossipee, 87, 88
Whitefield, 171
Wilmot, 99
Wilton, 40
Winchester, 34
Wolfeboro, 81
Wonalancet, 111, 113, 114
Connecticut Lakes Region,
    188–194
Cow Cave, 115
Crawford House, 126

Crawford Notch, 118, 125, 126,
    128, 133, 146
Crawford Notch Area, 125–134

Dartmouth College, 184, 185
Dartmouth–Lake Sunapee Region,
    90–109
Devil's Hopyard, 177, 179
Dixville Notch, 167, 185–188
Dixville Notch State Wayside Area,
    188
Dome Rock, 162
Dry River Valley, 132
Durand Ridge, 162
Eagle Cliff, 72, 73, 124
East Foss Farm, 23–25
East Inlet, 189, 192
Education centers. See SCIENCE/
    EDUCATION CENTERS
Elephant Head, 133
Errol Dam, 182
Evans Notch, 154, 155
Evans Notch Area, 154–157

FISH/SEA LIFE
    alewives, 56
    amphipods, 9
    bass, 8, 9, 56, 62, 64, 80
    bluefish, 9
    carp, 56
    copepods, planktonic, 2, 11
    crabs, 6, 9
    dolphins, 9
    eel, 2, 9

flounder, 9, 12–13
herring, river, 56
lobsters, 9, 12, 17
minnows, 8
mussels, dwarf wedge, 56–57
oysters, 9
perch, white, 62
pickerel, 62, 64
salmon, Atlantic, 55, 56
shrimp, 9
shad, 55, 56
shellfish, 9
silversides, 8
smelt, 8
trout, 56, 63
whales, 2, 9, 10, 11
FISHING
    in the Androscoggin River, 177
    in Big Squam Lake, 71, 72
    at Bretzfelder Memorial Park,
        170
    on Heald Pond, 40
    in Knight's Pond, 79, 81
    in Mount Sunapee State Park, 99
    in Pawtuckaway State Park,
        62–63
    in Pillsbury State Park, 96
    in South Pond Recreation Area,
        178
    at Stonedam Island, Lake
        Winnipesaukee, 76
    on Lake Umbagog, 184
    in White Lake, 87
    in White Mountain National
        Forest, 113
FLOWERS/PLANTS
    alpine plants, 30, 92, 130, 138,
        148

alyssum, 21
amaranthus, 21
arbutus, trailing, 88
asters, fall, 104
avens, mountain, 148
azaleas, 19, 94, 144, 148
begonias, 21
bilberry, alpine, 130, 148
"bird on the wing," 58
blueberries, 31, 32, 33, 34, 53, 70,
    72, 88
buckbean, 194
bulrush, northeastern, 57
celosia, 21
cinquefoil, 57, 138, 148
cloudberry, 130
columbine, 58, 152
coreopsis, 21
cotton, bog, 101
cowslips, 54
cranberry, mountain, 30, 138, 148
crowberry, black, 130,148
delphiniums, 104
diapensia, 148
dogwood, Chinese, 94
ferns, 19, 40, 50, 54, 60, 80, 88,
    100, 101, 106, 143, 144, 177
fungus, finger, 76
grapes, 20, 103
grass, tufted cotton, 30
hobblebush, 45
hollyhocks, 104
huckleberry, 72
impatiens, 21
iris, 20, 52, 104
Labrador tea, 101, 148
lady's slippers, 50, 54, 72, 144,
    145, 170

larkspurs, 21
laurel, bog, 88, 101
leatherleaf, 101, 102
lichen, 75-76
lilacs, 20, 21
lilies, 20
"love lies bleeding," 21
lupines, 50
marigolds, 21
mayflower, Canada, 152
milk-vetch, Jessup's, 57
moss, 101, 102, 178
nasturtiums, 21
orchid, small whorled pogonia,
    57
pansies, 21
peonies, 20, 103, 104
petunias, 21
phlox, 104
pitcher plant, 101, 102, 144, 172,
    194
pogonia, small whorled, 57
polygala, fringed, 58
poppies, 20, 21
rhododendrons, 19, 35, 94
rhodora, 37, 50
rock tripe, 75-76
rosebay, Lapland, 148
rosemary, bog, 101
roses, 13, 18, 19, 20, 21, 94
sandwort, mountain, 138, 153
sarsaparilla, 37
sedge, 101
silverling, 153
sundew plant, 102
Soloman's Seal, 20, 60
starflowers, 58
thistle, globe, 20

tithonia, 21
trillium, painted, 45
verbena, 21
violets, 54
wintergreen, 58, 152
wisteria, 19
zinnias, creeping, 21
Floating Island, 183–184
Flume, the, 134, 135, 188
FORESTS
Andorra Forest, 27, 31
Bartlett Experimental Forest, 121
Chamberlain-Reynolds Forest, 69
Connecticut Lakes State Forest, 189
Five-Finger Point, 72
Fox State Forest, 53–54
Gibbs Forst, 124
Heald Tract, 40
Kilkenny Region, 177
Kimball Wildlife Forest, 77–78
Madame Sherri Forest, 47–48
McCabe Forest, 41
Nash Stream State Forest, 181
old-growth forest (defined), 124
Peirce Wildlife and Forest Reservation, 27, 45
pitch-pine forest at White Lake State Park, 86, 87
Rhododendron State Park, 34–35
Sheiling State Forest, 39–40
Urban Forestry Center, 22
West Branch Pine Barrens, 86, 87, 88–89
White Mountain National Forest, 44, 48, 65, 111, 112–113, 121, 123, 124, 125, 130,

135, 146, 150, 154, 157, 158, 160, 167, 168, 172, 177, 188
Williams Family Forest, 46
Forest Service, U.S., 179
Franconia Notch, 124, 125, 133, 134, 136, 137, 141, 187
Franconia Notch Area, 134–137
Franconia Notch Parkway, 136
Franconia Ridge, 136, 148
Furber Strait, 8

GARDENS
on Appledore Island, 16, 21–22
at The Fells estate, 92, 94
Fuller Gardens, 18–19
"Garden of the Senses" (handicapped-accessible), 22
at Governor John Langdon House, 20
at Moffatt-Ladd House, 19–20
nature garden in Lost River Gorge, 143–144
in Prescott Park, 21
at Rundlet-May House, 20
at Saint-Gaudens National Historic Site, 103, 104, 105
at Wentworth-Coolidge Mansion, 20–21
at the Urban Forestry Center, 22
GEOLOGICAL FORMATIONS
felsenmeer creep (rock wave), 164
fir waves, 128, 129
fossil rock glacier, 164

giant boulders in Sherling State
Forest, 39–40
giant boulders in Pawtuckaway
State Park, 63
Giant Stairs, 132
glacial bowls, 34, 164
glacial cirques, 139, 146, 156,
164
glacial deposits, 30, 78, 79, 80,
89, 102
glacial erratics, 39–40, 63, 85,
86, 114, 147
glacial eskers ("horsebacks" or
"whalebacks"), 81, 83, 85,
126
glacial kettleholes, 53, 83, 85,
86
glacial potholes, 128
glacial ring dikes, 79
glacial striations, 99, 118, 123,
158
glacial trough, 134
Glen Boulder, 147
Madison Boulder, 86–87
outwash fan, 80, 89
pegmatite dikes, 143
Sarcophagus, the, 30
stoss and lee topography
("sheep's backs"), 126,
132–133, 149, 178
talus slope, 133
Also see ROCK FORMATIONS
Gibbs Brook Area, 124
Gorge (definition of), 143
Great Bay, 3, 5, 8, 9, 24, 25
Great Bay Estuarine Reserve, 2–6
Greeley Ponds Scenic Area,
123–125

Green Hills, 151
Green Hills Preserve, 152–154
"GREEN" ORGANIZATIONS
Appalachian Mountain Club, 98,
107, 112, 124, 125, 126,
127, 132, 146, 147, 149,
155, 156
Audubon Society of New
Hampshire, 3, 13, 14, 24,
25, 29, 32, 42, 51, 53, 56,
58, 59, 83, 84, 95, 108,
171, 172, 187
Chocorua Lake Conservation
Foundation, 85
Friends of the Wapack, 27, 37,
38
Great Bay Watch, 1
Harris Center, 31
Lakes Region Conservation
Trust, 67, 73, 74–75, 76, 81
Lake Sunapee Protective
Association, 91
Loon Preservation Committee,
77
Meriden Bird Club, 105, 106
Nature Conservancy, the, 57,
85, 88, 89, 152, 153, 154,
174, 181, 192, 194
New England Forestry
Foundation, 70
New Hampshire Natural
Heritage Inventory, 57
Randolph Mountain Club,
157–158, 162
Society for the Protection of
New Hampshire Forests
(Forest Society), 27, 30, 31,
32, 33, 41, 42, 46, 60, 61,

71, 91, 94, 98, 112, 113, 134, 142, 143, 144, 168, 169, 181
Squam Lakes Association, 67, 68, 71
Squam Lakes Conservation Society, 67, 69, 72
Unsworth Preserve Committee, 69
Wonalancet Outdoor Club, 113

Harvard Brook, 136
HIKING
in Bear Brook State Park, 63
to Eagle Cliff, 73
in Fox State Forest, 53
in Great Bay National Wildlife Refuge, 6, 7
near Harris Center for Conservation Education, 42, 45
in Heald Tract, 40
in the Kilkenny Region, 177
in King Ravine, 163–164
in Madame Sherri Forest, 48
in the Mahoosuc Range, 172
up Mount Kearsarge, 99, 100
near Mount Monadnock, 28, 30, 31, 32, 33
in Mount Sunapee State Park, 98, 99
up North Percy Peak, 182
in Pawtuckaway State Park, 64
in Pillsbury State Park, 96
in the Pinkham Notch Area, 146

in Wapack National Wildlife Refuge, 38
in Weeks State Park, 168
in White Mountain National Forest, 113, 134, 135
Horseback riding, 170
Howker Ridge, 162
HUNTING
in Bear Brook State Park, 63
near Knight's Pond, 81
in Pawtuckaway State Park, 64
in Lake Umbagog National Wildlife Refuge, 184
Huntington Cascades, 188
Huntington Ravine, 146

Insects, 49–50, 80, 87, 88
Imp Profile, 133, 147–148, 162
Indian Head, 135
ISLANDS
Appledore Island, 16, 17
Bowman Island, 70, 71
Diamond Island, 79
Duck Island, 17
Hog Island, 16
Horse Island, 64
Isles of Shoals, 15–18
Moon Island, 79–71
Rattlesnake Island, 79
Smuttynose Island, 17
Star Island, 16, 17
Stonedam Island, 67, 74–76
White Island, 16
Joblidunk Ravine, 139
Kancamagus Highway Area, 120–125

Kilkenny Region, 177
Kilkenny Ridge, 180-181
King Ravine, 124, 158, 163-165
Kinsman Notch, 107, 141, 144
Kinsman Notch Area, 137-144
Kinsman Ridge, 141, 143

LAKES
  Ammonoosuc Lake, 126-127
  Big Squam Lake, 67, 68, 69, 71,
    72, 73
  in Carter Notch, 149
  Chocorua Lake, 85, 113
  Connecticut Lakes, 167, 193
    First Connecticut Lake, 192
    Fourth Connecticut Lake, 194
  Dream Lake, 172
  Echo Lake, 134
  Kezar Lake, 100
  Lonesome Lake, 136, 137
  Newfound Lake, 107, 108, 109
  in Pawtuckaway State Park,
    63-64
  Purity Lake, 81
  Silver Lake, 83
  South Pond, 178-179
  Lake Sunapee, 90, 91, 92, 96,
    98
  Lake Umbagog, 118,167, 182,
    183
  White Lake, 83, 86, 87
  Lake Winnipesaukee, 67, 68,
    74, 76, 77, 78, 83
Lakes Region, 67-89
Leadmine Ledge, 175
Little Bay, 5, 8

Little Deer Hill, 155
Locke's Hill, 78
Logging operations, 112, 168, 180,
  181, 189, 193
Longstack precipice, 80
Lookoff Point, 143
Lookout Ledge, 162-163
Lost River, 141, 143
Lost River Gorge, 107, 142, 143
Lost River Reservation, 142-144
Lucia's Lookout, 96

Mascot Mine, 174
Merrimack Valley, 49-66
Monadnock Region, 27-48
Monadnock Reservation, 27, 30
Montalban Ridge, 120, 132
Mountain biking, 34, 53, 54, 63,
  64, 96
MOUNTAINS
  Abenaki Mountain, 186, 187
  Mount Adams, 133, 146, 154,
    157, 163
  Appalachians, the, 129
  Mount Ascutney, 103, 104
  Mount Avalon, 127
  Baldface Mountain, North, 155,
    156-157
  Baldface Mountain, South, 155,
    156-157
  Bald Mountain, 31-32, 134
  Belknap Mountain, 78-79, 83
  Black Cap, 151
  Black Mountain, 139
  Blueberry Mountain, 139
  Blue Job Mountain, 26

Bond Range, 122
Cannon Mountain, 133, 137
Mount Cardigan, 37, 98,
    106–107
Caribou Mountain, 154
Mount Carrigain, 132, 134, 154
Carter Dome, 120, 157, 162
Carter Range, 154, 175
Mount Chocorua, 84, 86, 111,
    113, 114, 118, 122, 123
Mount Clay, 146
Mount Clinton, 144
Mount Clough, 140
Mount Crawford, 131–132
Mount Crescent, 163
Crescent Range, 157, 162
Crotched Mountain, 36, 38, 96
Mount Deception, 127
Diamond Peaks, 184–185
Diamond Peak, West, 184
Dickey Mountain, 117, 118
Dome Rock, 162
Mount Doublehead, 150
Mount Dunstan, 184
Eastman Mountain, 156, 157
Mount Eisenhower, 126
Elephant Head, 133
Mount Field, 128
Mount Flume, 122
Franconia Range, 134, 171
Mount Franklin, 146
Mount Garfield, 129
Gap Mountain, 33
Mount Hale, 127
Mount Hayes, 175–176
Hedgehog Mountain, 121, 122
Horn, the, 180
Mount Israel, 114–115

Mount Jackson, 130–131
Mount Jefferson, 128, 146
Mount Kearsarge, 36, 37, 46,
    98, 99–100, 150
Kilkenny Region, 167, 168,
    177–181
Killington Mountain, 100
Kinsman Range, 134, 137
Mount Lafayette, 138
Little Monadnock, 35, 36
Long Mountain, 178
Lyndeborough Mountain, 37
Mount Madison, 146, 157, 158,
    163, 175
Magalloway Mountain, 192–193
Mahoosuc Range, 150, 167, 172,
    176, 179, 188
Mount Major, 79
Mount Mexico, 114
Moat Mountain, North, 150
Moat Range, 123
Mount Monadnock, 27, 29–30,
    31, 32, 33, 34, 36, 37, 44,
    45, 46, 47, 96, 98, 100
Mount Monroe, 133, 146
Mount Moosilaukee, 98, 135,
    138, 139, 140, 141
Nancy Mountain, 46
Mount Osceola, 119
Ossipee mountains, 79, 84
Owl's Head, 122, 187
Pack Monadnock, 35–36
Pack Monadnock, North, 36, 37,
    38
Mount Passaconaway, 86, 111,
    122, 123
Mount Paugus, 86, 111
Pawtuckaway Range, 63, 64

Peaked Mountain, 152, 153
Mount Pemigewasset, 135
Pind Mountain, 175
Pine Mountain, 158, 162
Mount Pisgah, 34
Pitcher Mountain, 31, 46
Pleasant Mountain, 144
Pliny Range, 171
Mount Potash, 121, 122
Presidential Range, 110, 130,
    132, 139, 146, 148,
    150,154, 158, 163, 171,
    175, 179, 181
Mount Prospect, 167, 168
Ragged Mountain, 98
Mount Randolph, 163
Rattlesnake Mountain, East, 71
Rattlesnake Mountain, West, 71
Rose Mountain, 37
Royce mountains, East and
    West, 157
Sandwich Mountain, 119, 135
Sandwich Range, 73, 84, 86,
    111, 115, 120, 122, 150
Scaur, the, 119
Skatutakee Mountain, 42, 44
Speckled Mountain, 154
Square Mountain, 187
Stairs Mountain, 132
Mount Stanton, 150
Mount Success, 176
Sugarloaf Mountain, 127, 182
Mount Sunapee, 37, 46, 98, 99
Table Mountain, 121
Table Rock, 186, 188
Mount Tecumseh, 119
Temple Mountain, 96
Three Sisters, 123

Thumb Mountain, 44
Mount Tom, 128
Mount Tripyramid, 119
Twin Mountain, North, 129
Twin Range, 171
Wantastiquet Mountain, 47
Mount Washington, 36, 100,
    120, 124, 125, 127, 128,
    132, 133, 138, 144, 146,
    147, 154, 162, 181
Mount Waumbek, 180
Mount Webster, 118, 125, 126
Webster Slide Mountain, 140
Welch Mountain, 117, 118
White Mountains, 17, 26, 83,
    106, 110–165
Whitewall Mountain, 130
Wildcat Mountain, 120, 162
Mount Willard, 125, 126, 127,
    128, 133
Mount Willey, 120, 125
Winn Mountain, 37
Mount Wonalancet, 113
Also see PEAKS
Mount Washington Cog Railway,
    125, 128, 129, 133, 144
Mount Washington Hotel, 125,
    128

Nash Stream, 182
Nash Stream Valley, 167, 181
National Natural Landmark, 171
National Scenic Byway, 120
"NATURAL AREAS"
    Bowl Research Natural Area,
    124

boulder field in Pawtuckaway State Park, 63
Stonedam Island Natural Area, 74–76
New Hampshire Department of Resources and Economic Development, 57
New Hampshire Division of Forests and Lands, 40, 48, 54, 181
New Hampshire Division of Parks and Recreation, 55, 66, 94, 107
New Hampshire Fish and Game Department, 3, 5, 6, 42, 65
New Hampshire Natural Heritage Inventory, 57, 153
New Hampshire, University of, 72, 78, 121
North Conway Area, 149–154
North Country, the, 166–194
Nowell Ridge, 158
Odiorne Point, 14, 17
"Old Man of the Mountains", 134
Outlook, the, 176

PARKS
Bear Brook State Park, 62–63
Bretzfelder Memorial Park, 170
Crawford Notch State Park, 125
Franconia Notch State Park, 134, 135
handicapped-accessible, 64, 66
Lake Francis State Park, 189
Miller State Park, 35–36

Monadnock State Park, 29, 33, 35
Mount Cardigan State Park, 106, 107
Northwood Meadows Pioneer Park, 64–66
Odiorne Point State Park, 12–13, 14
Pawtuckaway State Park, 63–64
Pillsbury State Park, 95–96, 99
Pisgah State Park, 27, 33–34
Prescott Park, 21
Rhododendron State Park, 34–35
Rollins State Park, 99, 100
Saint-Gaudens National Historic Site, 101–105
South Pond Recreation Area, 177, 178–179
Mount Sunapee State Park, 96–99
Wadleigh State Park, 100
Weeks State Park, 167–168
White Lake State Park, 86–87
Winslow State Park, 99, 100
Passaconaway Valley, 123
PEAKS
East Diamond Peak, 185
Firescrew Peak, 107
Jenning's Peak, 119
Noon Peak, 120
Percy Peak, North, 181, 182
Percy Peaks, 168,181–182
Percy Peak, South, 181
South Peak (on Mount Cardigan), 107
Whiteface Peak, 86
PEOPLE, FAMOUS
Carson, Rachel, 1

Thaxter, Celia, 16
Hassam, Childe, 16
Thoreau, Henry David, 29, 166
Muir, John, 110,146
Frost, Robert, 49, 54
Longfellow, Robert Wadsworth,
  51
McAuliffe, Chrissta, 61, 62
Saint-Gaudens, Augustus, 101,
  103, 104, 105
Weeks, John Wingate, 168
PICNICKING
  in Bear Brook State Park, 63
  in Bretzfelder Memorial Park,
    170
  on Caps Ridge Trail, 128
  in Chamberlain-Reynolds Forest,
    70
  in Fox State Forest, 54
  on Robert Frost Farm, 54
  in Lost River Reservation, 144
  near Meetinghouse Pond, 29
  in Miller State Park, 36
  in Monadnock State Park, 30
  in Mount Cardigan State Park,
    107
  near Mount Kearsarge, 100
  in Northwood Meadows Pioneer
    Park, 66
  in Odiorne Point State Park, 13
  in Pisgah State Park, 34
  in Rhododendron State Park, 35
  in Sheiling State Forest, 40
  in South Pond Recreation Area,
    178, 179
  on Star Island, 17
  at Stonedam Island, 76
  in Unsworth Preserve, 69

  at Upper Hill Pond, 117
  at Urban Forestry Center, 23
  in Weeks State Park, 168
  in White Lake State Park, 87
Pilot-Pliny Ridge, 180
Pinkham Notch, 133, 144, 146,
  147, 148, 175
Pinkham Notch Area, 144–149
PONDS
  on Appledore Island, 17
  Archery Pond, 62
  Bacon Pond, 96
  Basin Pond, 156
  Bear Hill Pond, 62
  Beaver Pond, 62, 141
  Black Fox Pond, 53
  Catamount Pond, 62
  Cherry Pond, Big, 171, 172
  Cherry Pond, Little, 172
  Cunningham Pond, 36
  East Pond, 118
  Fullam Pond, 34
  Gentian Pond, 172
  Great Turkey Pond, 58
  Greeley Ponds, 123, 124, 125
  Heald Pond, 40
  Heron Pond, 85
  Horseshoe Pond, 156
  Indian Pond, 47
  Knight's Pond, 79–81
  Leonard Pond, 184
  Lily Pond, 88
  Lost Pond, 146
  Mascot Pond, 173, 175
  Meader Pond, 140
  Meetinghouse Pond, 28–29
  Mountain Pond, 151
  Mud Pond, 140

Nancy Pond, 124
Page Pond, 172
in Pillsbury State Park, 96
Round Pond, 63
Shingle Pond, 150
South Pond, 178–179
Trout Pond, 46
Unknown Pond, 179
Upper Hall Pond, 117
Wachipauka Pond, 140
Willard Pond, 32
Portsmouth Harbor, 14, 16
Prospect House, 138

Red Bench Lookout, 126
Red Hill, 72, 73
Rines Hill, 80
RIVERS
Ammonoosuc River, 127
Androscoggin River, 162, 172,
176, 182–183, 184
Bellamy River, 25
Connecticut River, 47, 57, 139,
143, 167, 192, 194
Contoocook River, 37, 41
Dead Diamond River, 184, 193
Ellis River, 146
Johns River, 172
Lamprey River, 8
Magalloway River, 183, 184
Merrimack River, 3, 55, 60
Merrymeeting River, 79
Pemigewasset River, 122
Piscataqua River, 8
Squamscott River, 8
Swift Diamond River, 184

Swift River, 120
West Branch River, 88
Winnicut River, 8
ROCK FORMATIONS
Boott Spur, 147
Bridge of Sighs, 143
Elephant Head, 133
Glen Boulder, 147
Imp Profile, 133, 147–148, 162
Indian Head, 135
Old Man of the Mountains, 1134
Pinnacle Rock, 186
Pulpit Rock, 149
Rockclimbing, 154
Rocks, the, 168–170
Rogers Ledge, 179

Sagamore Creek, 23
Saint-Gaudens National Historic
Site, 101–105
Sandy Point, 5–6, 24
Sandwich Notch, 115, 116
Sanguinary Ridge, 186, 188
Scar Ridge, 122
SCIENCE/EDUCATION
CENTERS
Christa McAuliffe Planetarium,
61–62
Civilian Conservation Corps
museum, 63
Conservation Center, 59, 60
Fox State Forest museum, 54
Harris Center for Conservation
Education, 38, 42–45
Jackson Estuarine Research
Laboratory, 2, 5, 9

Land Studies Center at The Fells
    estate, 92
Mount Washington Observatory,
    133, 144, 164
Museum of Family Camping, 63
Paradise Point Nature Center,
    107–109
Rocks, the, 168–170
Sandy Point interpretive center,
    5, 6
Science Center of New
    Hampshire, 44, 73–74
Seacoast Science Center, 12, 13,
    15
Shoals Marine Laboratory, 16 18
Snowmobile Museum, 63
Stonedam Island environmental
    programs, 76
Weeks State Park programs, 168
Seacoast Region, 1–26
Signal Ridge, 132
SKIING, ALPINE
    at Cannon Mountain Ski Area,
        137
    at Mount Sunapee, 96, 99
    in Waterville Valley, 117
SKIING, CROSS-COUNTRY
    at The Balsams, 185
    in Bear Brook State Park, 63
    in Frank Bolles Nature Reserve,
        85
    on the Franconia Bike Path, 137
    in Great Bay National Wildlife
        Refuge, 7
    around Mount Monadnock, 30
    in Northwood Meadows Pioneer
        Park, 66
    in Odiorne Point State Park, 13

    in Pawtuckaway State Park, 64
    in Pillsbury State Park, 96
    in Pisgah State Park, 34
    around Mount Prospect, 168
    at The Rocks, 170
    in Wapack National Wildlife
        Refuge, 38
    in West Branch Pine Barrens, 89
    in White Lake State Park, 87
Sleeper Ridge, 111, 113
SNOWMOBILING
    in Bear Brook State Park, 63
    in the Connecticut Lakes Region,
        189
    on the Franconia Bike Path, 137
    in Pillsbury State Park, 96
    in Pisgah State Park, 34
SNOWSHOEING
    in Frank Bolles Nature Reserve,
        85
    near Meetinghouse Pond, 29
    in Northwood Meadows Pioneer
        Park, 66
    in Pillsbury State Park, 96
    at The Rocks,170
    in Wapack National Wildlife
        Refuge, 38
Snyder Brook, 162
Society for the Preservation of
    New England Antiquities,
    20
Southwest Corner Region, 167–172
Square Ledge, 146
Strawbery Banke, 21
Sunset Hill, 92
SWIMMING
    in Bear Brook State Park, 63
    in Big Squam Lake, 70

on Catamount Pond, 62
on Chocorua Lake, 85
in Mount Sunapee State Park, 99
in Pawtuckaway State Park, 64
in South Pond Recreation Area,
    178, 179
in Lake Umbagog National
    Wildlife Refuge, 184
in White Lake, 86, 87

Thirteen-Mile Woods (scenic
    drive), 176–177
TRAILS (by region)
  The Seacoast
    biking, 13
    up Blue Job Mountain, 26
    Brooks Trail, 22–23
    Great Bay National Wildlife
        Refuge, 6, 7
    handicapped-accessible, 22
    interpretive, 22
    in Odiorne Point State Park,
        13
    Turner Loop Trail, 6
    Woodman Point Trail, 6
  Monadnock Region
    around Bald Mountain, 32
    Cascade Link Trail, 30
    Harriskat Trail, 42
    in Heald Tract, 40, 41
    McCabe Forest nature trail, 41
    Metacomet-Monadnock Trail,
        33
    Monadnock-Sunapee
        Greenway, 31
    near Mount Monadnock, 29

along Old Chesterfield Road,
    34
around Pack Monadnock
    Mountain, 36
in Pisgah State Park, 34
up Pitcher Mountain, 31
Pumpelly Trail, 29, 30, 44
Rocky Ridge Trail, 28
in Sheiling State Forest, 39,
    40
Ski Trail, 46
Snowbrook Trail, 34
South Woods Trail, 34
Thumbs Up Trail, 42
Thumbs Down Trail, 45
Trout Bacon Trail, 45, 46
Wapack Trail, 36, 37
White Dot Trail, 29–30
Merrimack Valley
  in Bear Brook State Park, 62
  in Deering Wildlife Sanctuary,
      51
  Robert Frost Farm nature
      trail, 54
  in Northwood Meadows
      Pioneer Park, 66
  Pasture Trail, 71, 72
  in Pawtuckaway State Park,
      64
  in Ponemah Bog, 50
  wheelchair-accessible, 66
Lakes Region
  to Eagle Cliff, 73
  East Gilford Trail, 78
  East Rattlesnake Trail, 71–72
  Esker Trail, 81
  Five-Finger Point, 72
  interpretive, 74

through Kimball Wildlife
Forest, 78
Old Bridle Path, 71
Ridge Trail, 71
in the Squam Lakes Area, 68,
71
on Stonedam Island, 74, 75,
76
through Thompson Bird
Sanctuary and Wildlife
Refuge, 84
around White Lake, 86
Dartmouth–Lake Sunapee
Region
Bear Pond Trail, 96
Elwell Trail, 108
John Hay National Wildlife
Refuge nature trail, 91,
92
Lakeside Trail, 108
Mad Road Trail, 96
Monadnock-Sunapee
Greenway Trail, 95, 96, 98,
99
up Mount Kearsarge, 99
Newbury Trail, 98
Pamac Trail, 96
through Philbrick-Cricenti
Bog, 100–101
Rim Trail, 98, 137
through Saint-Gaudens
National Historic Site, 104
Solitude Trail, 98
West Ridge Trail, 106, 107
The White Mountains
Ammonoosuc Ravine Trail,
129
Around-the-Lake Trail, 126

Around-Lonesome-Lake Trail,
137
Attitash Trail, 121
Baldface Circle Trail, 157
Baldface Knob Trail, 157
up Bald Mountain, 134
Basin-Cascade Trail, 136, 137
Basin Rim Trail, 156
Basin Trail, 156
Beaver Brook Trail, 141
Benton Trail, 138
Big Pines Path, 119
Big Rock Cave Trail, 114
Black Cap Path, 151
Black Mountain Trail, 139
Boulder Loop Interpretive
Trail, 123
Brook Trail, 114
Cabin Trail, 114
Caps Ridge Trail, 128
Carrigain Notch Trail, 134
Cascade Brook Trail, 136
Champney Falls Trail, 114
Chippewa Trail, 139
Conant Trail, 155
Crawford Path, 124
Crescent Ridge Trail, 163
Davis Path, 132
up Dome Rock, 162
Dry River Trail, 148
East Branch Truck Road, 122
East Pond Trail, 118
ecology path in Lost River
Reservation, 142
to Elephant Head, 126
Franconia Ridge Trail, 134
to Georgiana and Harvard
Falls, 136

to Glen Boulder, 147
Glencliff Trail, 139
Gorge Brook Trail, 138, 139
Greeley Ponds Trail, 119
Guinea Pond Trail, 115
up Hedgehog Mountain,
    121–122
Imp Trail, 147–148
Indian Head Trail, 135
Inlook Trail, 162
Kettles Path, 119
King Ravine Trail, 163–164
Ledge Trail, 158, 163
Liberty Trail, 113
Lincoln Woods Trail, 122
up Little Deer and Big Deer
    hills, 155–156
Livermore Trail, 119
Lonesome Lake Trail, 136
Lost Pond Trail, 146
Mead Trail, 115
Moosilaukee Carriage Road,
    139
Mountain Pond Loop Trail,
    151
up Mount Chocorua, 114
Mount Kearsarge North Trail,
    150
up Mount Moosilaukee, 141
Mount Pemigewasset Trail,
    135
Nineteen-Mile Brook Trail,
    149
Old Paugus Trail, 114
Peaked Mountain Path, 152
Pine-Lord-Harndon Trail, 155
up Pine Mountain, 158
Piper Trail, 114

in the Randolph area, 158
Sandwich Mountain Trail, 119
in Sandwich Range
    Wilderness Area, 113
Sargent Path, 162–163
Scaur Trail, 119
Short Line Trail, 164
up Signal Ridge, 132
Skookumchuck Trail, 137
Slippery Brook Trail, 157
Snapper Trail, 139
up South Baldface Mountain,
    156, 157
along Tunnel Brook, 139–140,
    141
Webster Cliff Trail, 130
Weeks Brook Trail, 150
Welch-Dickey Loop Trail, 117
Wentworth Trail, 115
Willard Trail, 127
Zealand Trail, 129
The North Country
    up to the Diamond Peaks, 184,
        185
    in the Dixville Notch area,
        185, 186, 188
    Four Seasons Trail, 170
    to Fourth Connecticut Lake,
        194
    to Garfield Falls, 193
    to Mount Hayes, 173
    Kilkenny Ridge Trail, 177,
        179, 180–181
    up Magalloway Mountain,
        192–193
    Mahoosuc Trail, 172, 173
    to Mascot Pond, 173
    around Mount Prospect, 168

up North Percy Peak, 182
North-South Heritage Trail,
  168
in Pondicherry Refuge, 171,
  172
Return Loop Trail, 169
along Sanguinary Ridge, 186,
  188
in South Pond Recreation
  Area, 178-179
Success Trail, 176
on Sugarloaf Mountain, 182
up Table Rock, 186
to Unknown Pond, 179
Woodland Trail, 169
TREES
  apple, 53
  arborvitae, 19
  ash, green, 60
  aspen, 23, 41, 78, 121, 124
  balsam, 48, 118, 131, 160, 161,
    169, 171, 178, 193
  beech, 48, 118, 151, 152, 177
  birch, 28, 48, 58, 80, 99, 118,
    121, 124, 130, 151, 178,
    180, 190
  cherry, 53
  crabapple, Japanese, 21
  fir, 47, 48, 94, 118, 121, 125,
    130, 131, 138, 160, 161,
    166, 168, 169, 178, 180,
    182, 189, 193
  fruit trees, 19, 53
  hawthorn, 53
  hazelnut, American, 23
  hemlock, 28, 37, 39, 53, 75, 77,
    84, 103, 107, 108, 124, 126,
    160, 178

horse chestnut, 19
locust, honey, 104
maple, 41, 47, 48, 58, 62, 75,
  92, 100, 106, 118, 151, 177,
  190
mulberry, white, 39
oak, 26, 28, 50, 52-53, 58, 60,
  72, 78, 88, 89, 152
pine, 3, 6, 22, 28, 37, 39, 48,
  49, 50, 58, 60, 71, 72, 78,
  80, 86, 87, 88, 89, 92, 103,
  117, 118, 151, 152, 160,
  170, 180
poplar, 80, 190
sassafras, 45, 48
spruce, 46, 47, 48, 101, 102,
  121, 125, 131, 138, 147,
  151, 156, 161, 166, 168,
  177, 178, 182, 192, 193,
  194
sumac, staghorn, 13, 23
tamarack (larch), 48, 101, 102,
  161
tupelo, 53, 72
Tuckerman Ravine, 146
Tunnel Brook, 139

University of New Hampshire, 23,
  25
Unknown Pond Brook, 180
U.S. Fish and Wildlife Service, 7
WALKING
  in Frank Bolles Nature Reserve,
    85
  in Deering Wildlife Sanctuary,
    53

in Fox State Forest, 54
in Great Bay Estuarine Reserve, 5
at the Harris Center, 42, 45
in John Hay National Wildlife Refuge, 94
around Knight's Pond, 80, 81
near Meetinghouse Pond, 29
on Moon and Bowman islands, 71
in Odiorne Point State Park, 13
in Pawtuckaway State Park, 64
in Rhododendron State Park, 35
in Sheiling State Forest, 40
on Star Island, 17
in Unsworth Preserve, 69
in the Urban Forestry Center, 23
WATERFALLS
Beaver Brook Cascades, 141
Beede Falls, 115
near Dome Rock, 162
Flume, the, 134, 135, 188
Garfield Falls, 193–194
Georgiana Falls, 135–136
Glen Ellis Falls, 147
Harvard Falls, 136
Huntington Cascades, 188
Kinsman Falls, 136
in Lost River Reservation, 143
Lower Falls, 127
Paradise Falls, 143
Pearl and Beecher cascades, 127
Rocky Glen Falls, 136
Thoreau Falls, 130
Waterville Valley, 117, 119, 123
whale-watching, 9–12
Whiteface Brook, 132
White Hills, 163

White Horse Ledge, 133, 153
White Ledge, 87
White Ledges, 98
White Mountains Region, 110–165
Whites Ledge, 150
WILDERNESS AREAS
Caribou–Speckled Mountain Wilderness, 116
definition of, 116
Great Gulf Wilderness Area, 116, 124, 146
Pemigewasset Wilderness Area, 116, 122, 129, 150
Presidential–Dry River Wilderness, 116, 146
Sandwich Range Wilderness Area, 111–117, 119, 122, 124
WILDLIFE AREAS/REFUGES
in Bear Brook State Park, 63
Bellamy River Wildlife Sanctuary, 25
bird sanctuaries, 65, 83–84
Frank Bolles Nature Reserve, 83, 84–86
Chase Sanctuary, 58
Deer Hill Bog Wildlife Viewing Blind, 155
Deering Wildlife Sanctuary, 51–53
DePierrefeu-Willard Pond Wildlife Sanctuary, 31–32
East Foss Farm, 23–25
Great Bay National Wildlife Refuge, 2, 3, 6–7
Harris Center for Conservation Education, 42–45

John Hay National Wildlife
    Refuge, 91–94
Hebron Marsh Wildlife
    Sanctuary, 108–109
Hoyt Wildlife Sanctuary, 81–83
Kimball Wildlife Forest, 77–78
Frederick and Paula Anna
    Markus Sanctuary, 76–77
Merrimack River Outdoor
    Education Area and
    Conservation Center, 59–61
Peirce Wildlife and Forest
    Reservation, 45–47
Pondicherry Refuge, 171
Scotland Brook Sanctuary, 172
Silk Farm Wildlife Sanctuary,
    56–59

Smith Pond Bog, 59
Helen Woodruff Smith
    Sanctuary, 105–106
Stoney Brook Wildlife
    Sanctuary, 95
Thompson Bird Sanctuary and
    Wildlife Refuge, 83–84
Lake Umbagog National Widlife
    Refuge, 182–184
Unsworth Preserve, 68–69
Wapack National Wildlife
    Refuge, 36–39
wheelchair-accessible, 83–84
Willey House Historic Site,
    125
Woodman Point, 3
Zealand Notch, 128–130